Edward Cline

BOARDING PARTIES
&
GRAPPLING HOOKS

Critical Sorties and Forays

In the War of Ideas

Patrick Henry Press

Library of Congress Cataloguing-in-Publication Data

Edward Cline (1946 -)
Boarding Parties & Grappling Hooks/Edward Cline

ISBN-13: 978-1482087833
ISBN-10: 1482087839

Patrick Henry Press, Williamsburg, Virginia

Cover Illustration: The French *Bayonnaise*'s crew boarding the British HMS *Ambuscade*, December 1798, by Louis-Philippe Crépin, Musée national de la Marine

Publisher's Note: This book is a collection of essays and commentaries originally published on Rule of Reason, blog site for the Center for the Advancement of Capitalism, and in other venues. They are copyrighted by the author.

Table of Contents

Foreword

Foreword

    This is the fourth anthology of commentaries and essays collected from Rule of Reason and other weblogs over the years. They focus on current politics, Islam, freedom of speech, various cultural issues, and miscellaneous subjects. The startling and unexpected reelection of Barack Obama in 2012 for another four years to continue what frankly should be deemed a nihilist campaign to "deconstruct" America should cause anyone who values his freedom and his life to enter into a state of permanent trepidation. Much has happened since the publication of *Corsairs & Freebooters* in 2012: the Benghazi massacre, in which a U.S. ambassador was murdered, together with his three companions, a policy disaster for which neither the president nor the secretary of state takes responsibility; a concerted assault on gun ownership and on freedom of speech, in violation of the Second and First Amendments, by the government, the Mainstream Media, and Islamic supremacists; the mounting multi-trillion dollar federal debt, which can never be paid; and the penchant of the new incumbent president to rule by "executive order," which obviates one check on federal power so carefully and conscientiously devised by the Founders as a check on tyranny.

    I grapple with these and other matters as cathartic exercises to stave off the viral malaise of hopelessness that seems to have crippled the spirit of the country. Otherwise, I should be locked in a state-owned rubber room and constrained by a straightjacket. My method is to attack without mercy, without hesitation, to slash and cut in a whirlwind of fury, to bring down as many of the enemy crew as possible.

    Long Live Lady Liberty.

Edward Cline
Williamsburg, Virginia
January 2013

Freedom of Speech

A Monument to the Death of Literature

In July, the editorial board of *The Modern Library*, a division of Random House, released their ranked list of the "one hundred greatest English-language novels of the 20th century." First on the list was James Joyce's *Ulysses*. The board could not have chosen a more fitting symbol of this century's dismal cultural legacy.

Joyce was awarded two more places on the list, for *Finnegan's Wake* and *A Portrait of the Artist as a Young Man*. Many of the "usual suspects" of the literary establishment are also present on the list, including J.D. Salinger's *The Catcher in the Rye*, Sinclair Lewis's *Main Street*, and William Golding's *Lord of the Flies*. Henry James, George Orwell, E.M. Forster, Joseph Conrad, D.H. Lawrence, and William Faulkner also garnered multiple citations. Detective novels were represented by Dashiell Hammett's *The Maltese Falcon*, while the sole semi-Romantic novel, Rudyard Kipling's *Kim*, came in at number seventy-eight.

As a selection of the best literary efforts of the century, the *Modern Library* list is tellingly dreary. It is dominated largely by exponents of Naturalism, the school which eschews portrayals of volitional, efficacious, heroic man – man as he might be and ought to be – to dwell on deterministic, helpless, miserable man – man as he allegedly is. On the list also is a significant corps of execrable writers who portray man as absurd, futile, or evil.

1

Many of the Naturalists on the list, however, were far better writers than Joyce; despite their corrupt view of man; these writers still adhered to the role and rules of language as a means of communicating ideas and telling a story. In terms of writing ability, excellence of style, or the stature of their characters, a half-dozen writers on the *Modern Library* list make Joyce look like a semi-literate brute.

Why, then, was *Ulysses*, a novel about "the little people" that can be read only in an out-of-focus trance, picked to occupy first place on the list?

Historically, *Ulysses* was the literary expression of the modern art movement, which ascended with Impressionism in the late 19th century, ten spiraled downward, out of fuel, to a splattering, pilotless crash that has left us with the slashes, gashes, and fused wreckage that today passes for art. While the Dadaists and other "rebels" were dispensing with the formal attributes, materials, and disciplines of art – in music, sculpture, painting, and drama – Joyce discarded all the requirements of writing: plot, structure, grammar, intelligibility, and, above all, volitional, goal-directed characters. For these, he substituted a studied "spontaneous" method of narrative and dialogue, otherwise known as the "stream of consciousness" style of writing. Joyce did not pioneer this style; he and his defenders merely made it acceptable.

While *Ulysses* contains fictional characters and events, it defies any rational attempt to define its story, structure, or purpose. Its pornographic and scatological elements, shocking in the first third of the century (the book was banned in the U.S. until 1934), are tame by today's standards, its episodic, lottery-style, unconnected events, its incessant trite patter and internal dialogue, and its smugly concrete-bound characters have less reality and invoke less interest than the worst daytime television soap opera. The novel is merely a collection of meandering reveries by nonentities on an exhausting number of trivial matters, all expressing a single theme: the irrelevancy of everything.

Here is just a brief excerpt, chosen at random:

> You move a motion? Steve, boy, you're going it some. More bluggy drunkables? Will immensely splendiferous stander permit one stooder of most extreme poverty and one largesize grandacious thirst to terminate one expensive inaugurated libation? Give's a breather. Landlord, have you good wine, Staboo? Hoots, mon, wee drap to pree. Cut and come again. Right

Boniface! Absinthe the lot. *Nos omnes biberimus viridum toxicum diabolus capiat posterioria nostra.* Closing-time, gents. Eh? Rome boos for the Boom toff. I hear you say onions? Bloo? Codges ads? Photo's papli, by all that's gorgeous!*

And so on. This is one of the more comprehensible passages; one can guess that it has something to do with drinking. The last soliloquy in the original edition is forty-five pages long – without a single paragraph break or punctuation mark. Imagine an amalgam of the prime-time hit, "Ally McBeal," the "adult" animated cartoon series, "Beavis and Butt-Head," and "The Jerry Springer Show," all transcribed somehow into literary terms, and you will have a sense of the spirit and content of Joyce's magnum opus. *Qua* literature, the novel is a vile fraud perpetrated by Joyce and by the same species of intellectual dishonesty and hatred for the good that foisted Picasso and his ilk on the public. *Ulysses* can only be considered "best" by a standard that consists of the destruction of standards – that is, by the standard of nihilism.

Yet from the first, *Ulysses* was deemed by critics and intellectuals to be so rich in profundity that it instantly acquired the status of a "classic," and it is now required reading in most college literature courses. Countless scholars have devoted whole careers to interpreting *Ulysses* and other works by Joyce, emending their sentences to conform to original manuscript versions and placing all their minutiæ under the microscope of "textual analysis" in order to write tens of thousands of pages of explication – not one of which sheds any light on what the novel is about.

"It is not the best novel," admits Joe Kidd, director of the James Joyce Research Center at Boston University. "It is simply the most influential novel."** But this novel by itself could not have exerted any influence on the culture – not even with its notoriety as a banned book – without the collusion of the culture's intellectuals, critics, and academics. "The book came at a time when the 19th century novel form, with his omniscient narrator, was exhausted," explains Dimitia Smith in The New York Times. "Where once the novel had been the story of heroes, it was now about the struggles of the common man."*** Exhausted? Say, rather, *murdered* – by Kant and his 20th century trustees in the realm of esthetics, by those who opposed the idea that a novel should be intelligible and that its subject should be man the hero.

The reason that *Modern Library* chose *Ulysses* as the best novel of the 20th century is that, on the deepest level, it was the most consistent example of the spirit common to the rest of the list. Most of the other novels selected for the list are merely more genteel, palatable, literate expressions of the philosophy behind Joyce's work, the philosophy that sees man as a pathetic, irrational creature ruled by his demons, emotions, and irreconcilable conflicts. Measured by this standard, Joyce's novel is pure, consistent Naturalism, unrestrained by any concession to focus, clarity, logic, continuity, or even character development. By this standard, the best sentence in Sinclair Lewis's Main Street (which ranked sixty-eighth) is inferior to the worst sentence in *Ulysses*, precisely because it has a value and a purpose within the context of Lewis's story. Lewis's purpose was not to assault the readers' minds with premeditated irrationality and to destroy literary standards, but that *was* Joyce's purpose.

If it was to remain consistent with its philosophical premises, the *Modern Library*'s board could not do other than to choose *Ulysses* as the best novel of the 20th century. Nor is it surprising that the Modern Library list gave no recognition to either *The Fountainhead* or *Atlas Shrugged* – which are in fact the two best novels of this century. The best in man is absolutely invisible and literally incredible to men whose sight is transfixed by the "realism" of the sewer.

As it stands, the *Modern Library* list is a fitting monument to the self-destruction of literature in the past century – and a full demonstration of the desperate need for its rebirth in the 21st century.

*James Joyce, *Ulysses*, 1921 (Random House, New York, 1934), p. 419.
**Quoted in "Why They Invented Cliffs Notes," New York Times, July 26, 1998.
***Ibid.

(This article first appeared in The *Intellectual Activist*, September 1998, Vol. 12, No. 9)

March 2012

Freedom of Speech: Silence is Not Golden

One demonstrable "toxic asset" of the country's governing altruist philosophy comes in two forms: censorship and the "fairness doctrine," or the suppression of free speech and its regulation. Of course, "regulated" speech cannot be free, either; regulation is simply an overture to censorship. Call it "Censorship Lite." While in the economic realm the federal government is actively and noisily nationalizing the economy, the move to de facto censorship has recently bolted ahead, as well, from a fast walk to a gallop on padded hooves to better steal up on us and lop off our heads. Distracted by the gutting of Wall Street and the ongoing vilification of all business CEOs, and not just those who were seduced by the chance to profit from subprime mortgages, few people are paying attention to the peril in which their right to speak against Congress and the administration has been put.

The cyclone of legislation and engineered destruction of freedom and capitalism being whipped up by President Barack Obama and the Democratic Congress (the Republicans, a.k.a. the GOP, or Grand Old Pathetics, as I am want to call them, no longer can be said to count for opposition to anything) cannot help but be accompanied by an aggressive assault on the freedom of speech to suppress all spoken and written dissent and opposition, to silence those whose ideas the administration and Congress do not want to hear and do not want others to hear. This assault represents the logical amalgamation of Left and Right.

Historically, and by necessity, one of the first casualties of a collectivist "revolution," such as we are witnessing today, has been the free press by either its complete abolition or its takeover by the usurpers. The goal of such physical force serves a number of purposes: to silence those whose ideas are a threat to the totalitarians' ideological and economic hegemony; to impose conformity on the public, and thus create a population of passive, yeah-saying or silent slaves; to regulate the minds of the public by suffocating them with propaganda and with a fear of the consequences of open, public dissent.

In such circumstances, the guiltiest party is a "free" press which voluntarily parrots the government line, either from agreement with the government's ends or from ignorance. The American news media today can be charged with a combination of both offenses.

But Congress and the federal government are not the only parties stealing a march on the First Amendment of the Constitution. The Jerusalem Post of March 12 reported:

"The Islamic states circulated a new resolution at the current session of the U.N. Human Rights Council in Geneva on Wednesday that could criminalize defamation of Islam as a human rights violation and encourage the imposition of Sharia.

"According to the nonbinding governmental resolution, titled 'Combating Defamation of Religions,' anything deemed insulting to Islamic sensitivities would be banned as a 'serious affront to human dignity' and a blatant violation of religious freedom."

The Post reports that the only religion named in the resolution is Islam.

Of course, given the moral relativism of the Obama administration (not to mention that of the Bush administration), such a "law" would be granted legitimacy if it ever came to having to take an official position on Islam. "Defaming" Islam by identifying its brutal, anti-mind nature, by cataloging the crimes committed in its name, by highlighting the *Koran*'s invitation to murder, genocide and enslavement, and by reporting its pathological hatred of freedom and free minds and its barbarous conduct towards its own adherents, can be deemed "criminal." It is the brother of secular "hate speech." And the fact that hate speech laws exist in several states and are condoned by the judiciary does not bode well for anyone who wishes to tackle the issue of jihad.

"Introduced by Pakistan on behalf of the Organization of Islamic Conference (OIC), it passed by a 108-51 margin, with 25 abstentions....The resolution decries 'the negative projection of Islam in the media' and voices 'deep concern that Islam is frequently and wrongly associated with human rights violations and terrorism.'"

I cannot recall the last time any member of the news media "negatively projected" Islam. Nor can I recall the last time the news media reported any of Islam's "human rights" violations, either abroad or here in the U.S., such as the "honor" killings of teenage girls who stray from the deadening Muslim subculture. The news media's knee-jerk deference to all things Muslim is rooted in non-judgmental fear. The Western press has been intimidated and practices self-censorship. Pakistan is an alleged ally of the U.S. in the war against the Taliban in Afghanistan. The resolution was also supported by our other "allies," Egypt and Iraq. It is payback for all the billions of dollars in aid the U.S. has sent to those countries.

A more visceral method of censorship occurred in Fairfax County, Virginia, when over 600 Muslims packed an auditorium for a hearing of the county planning commission on whether or not to allow a Saudi Wahhabist school (or a mind-killing, anti-Western madrassa) to expand on property already leased to it by the county. The commissioners extended every courtesy to the Muslim mob, and none to the few who questioned the wisdom of allowing an incubator of jihad to grow in the "community," who were bullied, shouted down, and surrounded by hostile Muslims with the sanction of the commissioners.

The Virginia of Patrick Henry, Thomas Jefferson, George Mason and James Madison -- the colony and state in the intellectual forefront of championing individual rights and limited government -- is not the Virginia that exists today. Its governor not only endorsed Obama and signed a bill banning smoking in bars and restaurants (in an exercise of eminent domain, or the partial seizure of property to benefit others), but went begging to Washington for a cut of the stimulus billions.

Here in the U.S., the federal government and its enablers in Congress are working frantically to suppress or discourage any kind of speech they deem "offensive" or "unfair."

"Senior FCC staff working with acting Federal Communications Commissioner Michael Copps held meetings last week with policy and legislative advisers to House Energy and Commerce Committee Chairman Henry Waxman to discuss ways the committee can create openings for the FCC to put in place a form of the 'Fairness Doctrine' without actually calling it such."

Waxman, one of the most power-lusting congressmen in politics, who also wants tobacco put under Food and Drug regulation, and who is practically a caricature of an Ayn Rand villain, "is also interested, say sources, in looking at how the Internet is being used for content and speech purposes."

"One idea Waxman's committee staff is looking at is a congressionally mandated policy that would require all TV and radio stations to have in place 'advisory boards' that would act as watchdogs to ensure 'community needs and opinions' are given fair treatment. Reports from those advisory boards would be used for license renewals and summaries would be reviewed at least annually by FCC staff."

Those "advisory boards" would function as the Politburo did in Soviet Russia, to enforce compliance with federal criteria of what constituted "community needs" and to decide whose opinions were to be given "fair treatment." (Are you ready for an all-Muslim version of "Dancing with the Stars" or a La Raza-approved interpretation of the Alamo?) Forgotten by the likely victims of this looming legislation is the fact that the FCC is already a component of the welfare state, having the authority to ration out the airwaves to the highest bidders and those with political pull in the name of "public service."

The Internet poses a particular threat to the statists, because it can now replace not only newspapers and the airwaves, but serves as an alternative to those media for information, opinion, and objective journalism. The Waxman-Pelosi-Reid-Obama coalition and its allies wish to regulate it and tax it. The Internet cannot be controlled and taxed except by either the FCC or another, newer government body. Google, Yahoo, Microsoft Outlook and other Internet "providers" or "common carriers" could be forced to have "advisory boards," as well. And given their cooperation with totalitarian regimes such as China's, not much opposition to regulation should be expected from them.

For an excellent comment on the rise and possible fate of the Internet under Obama, see Charles Festel's Titanic Deck Chairs site here.

From rationing out the airwaves, a power it should not have, the government may be moving to rationing out newsprint.

"With many U.S. newspapers struggling to survive, a Democratic senator on Tuesday [March 24] introduced a bill to help them by allowing newspaper companies to restructure as nonprofits with a variety of tax breaks.

"Cardin's [Benjamin Cardin] Newspaper Revitalization Act would allow newspapers to operate as nonprofits for educational purposes under the U.S. tax code, giving them a similar status to public broadcasting systems [that is, to the various units of the Corporation for Public Broadcasting system, or PBS]."

There is an instance of beggar thy looting neighbor.

"Cardin's office said his bill was aimed at preserving local and community newspapers, not conglomerates which may also own radio and TV stations. His bill would also let a nonprofit buy newspapers owned by a conglomerate."

Except for government departments and agencies, *big* is always "bad." And here is the logical catch to winning a government-granted "nonprofit" status:

"Under this arrangement, newspapers would still be free to report on all issues, including political campaigns. But they would be prohibited from making political endorsements. Advertising and subscription revenue would be tax-exempt, and contributions to support news coverage or operations could be tax deductible."

And there you have it. Newspapers bailed out through the ruse of being dubbed "nonprofit" organizations would be required to gag themselves, in exchange for tax-exemptions on their revenue. The power to *not* tax can be as destructive as the power to tax, if the bribe or inducement is tempting enough to those who do not think ahead or who do not care to think at all. Of course, that would leave TV, radio, and the Internet as sources of news and opinions Americans want to search for, read or hear, and not what politicians and the government would prefer them to read or hear.

Theoretically, Americans would be compelled to listen to opposing viewpoints and opinions under a resuscitated "Fairness Doctrine," a mongrel concept that purports to advance "diversity" in politics and culture but which was declared unconstitutional by the FCC in 1987 and abandoned. In reality, Americans would not listen to or watch what the government and "public service" advocates wished them to audit. The failure of Air America, a left-liberal radio station created to counter popular conservative talk radio, testifies to the power of volition. Radio stations across the country did not wish to syndicate or carry Air America because their owners or managers knew that their audiences did not wish to listen to it. (Americans already get enough of left-liberal perspectives and talking points in their newspapers and from politicians.)

"Senator Debbie Stabenow, D-Mich., told radio host Bill Press yesterday when asked about whether it was time to bring back the so-called 'Fairness Doctrine': 'I think it's absolutely time to pass a standard. Now, whether it's called the Fairness Standard, whether it's called something else -- I absolutely think it's time to be bringing accountability to the airwaves....'"

Which means: Any station that allows someone like Rush Limbaugh to publicly hope that Obama's policies fail, would be held "accountable" and presumably penalized, taken over, or driven out of business. Stabenow, John Kerry, Nancy Pelosi and their cohorts are not working to see Rush Limbaugh debate someone like Bill Moyers (of PBS) on important issues; they know that Limbaugh, whatever his faults, would wipe the floor with Moyers and that countless Americans would cheer Limbaugh on with all the raucous gusto of a crowd watching a prize fight. The last thing the advocates of "fairness" and "balance" want is *confrontation*. They know they would lose.

But the fundamental purpose of the "Fairness Doctrine," or whatever its new name might be, is not to establish "fair standards" or to enforce 'accountability" or to "serve" the public. Its goal is to destroy the very concept of free speech, to reduce it to a contest of "he said-she said," to give insupportable, arbitrary assertions the same weight as statements of fact -- in short, to sully the value of the freedom of speech, to nullify the role of ideas and to inculcate in one's mind a cloying indifference to whatever anyone says about anything.

In June a ruling is expected from the Supreme Court on whether or not a documentary film, "Hillary: The Movie," produced by a conservative group, Citizens United, is political speech or a political ad. It was shown in eight theaters during the primaries in 2008 and intended to criticize Hillary Clinton, then regarded as the favorite to win the Democratic nomination. The Federal Election Commission subsequently prohibited it from being aired on television.

"Government lawyers argued that conservative group Citizens United's 90-minute documentary…is a political ad just like traditional one-minute or 30-second spots and therefore regulated by the McCain-Feingold law, the popular name for 2002 revisions to the nation's campaign finance laws [the Bipartisan Campaign Reform Act].

> "The FEC's conclusion that the movie was nothing more than an overt attempt to persuade voters not to side with Hillary Clinton was affirmed by a three-judge panel last summer which ruled the film had 'no other interpretation' other than as an advocacy message to voters that Clinton should not be elected."

Whether or not the Court rules for or against the film, its decision will likely be grounded on non-fundamental reasons. The Court will not challenge the validity of McCain-Feingold, only the utterly arbitrary rules by which it is enforced and whether or not they are practical or "fair." It will not venture to rule McCain-Feingold and every other statutory or legislative abridgement of the First Amendment unconstitutional. It will simply count beans and measure concretes and second-guess the intent of the film and of its producers.

Helping the Court dodge the issue is Citizens United itself:

"Citizens United appealed to the Supreme Court, arguing that 'Hillary: The Movie' should not be considered a political ad. The group says there is nothing in the movie urging people to vote against Clinton. The group says the film is more of a documentary comparable to critical television news programs such as 'Frontline,' 'Nova,' and '60 Minutes.'"

No political principle I know of was ever defended by artful insinuation, which is what the group's argument before the Court amounts to. "It really isn't what you think it is, it's something else entirely, and shouldn't be called a political ad. It is an 'express advocacy' of nothing. Clinton just happens to be the subject."

Cringing is not an efficacious method of persuasion. Far be it from Citizens United to insist that the government has an obligation to defend anyone's right to persuade voters about candidates and issues in any style or medium he wishes or thinks the most effective, at any time before, during, and after a campaign, paid for with as much funding as possible by whatever any individual or group is willing to provide it. Far be it from Citizens United to insist that the Court uphold the First Amendment.

With friends like that, freedom of speech does not need enemies.

March 2009

Cass Sunstein: "Czar" in Wolf's Clothing

In "Reason is Forever" I commented on the phenomenon of liberals, collectivists, and fascist/socialist fellow travelers in the Obama administration endorsing the gagging of anyone who criticizes the administration and its agenda, and wishing to bestow a taxpayer-bought bullhorn on Obama's propagandists. I also discuss the incremental move to censorship in America in "Censorship by Nickels and Dimes," "Thought Crime: The Logical End of Politically Correct Speech," and "The Move Towards Freedomless Speech."

The National Endowment for the Arts (NEA) was recently caught with its curtain drawn open for its role in that effort. Its director of communications, Yosi Sergant, was the facilitator of a teleconference of artists and other "cool people" who had not only benefited from NEA grants, but worked directly or indirectly to elect Obama. The ostensive purpose of the call was to enlist the active support of the invited participants to "sell" the Obama agenda, including the health-care bill, to the public. It took a while for the implications of that "call to arms" to sink into the consciousness of Patrick C. Courrielche, columnist for Big Hollywood, who subsequently, and with some apparent regret, reported the call in detail on the Big Hollywood blog site.

For having violated its nominally apolitical mandate (if it is a creature of politics, how could it be "apolitical"?), the NEA went mum after the whistle-blowing, and the director of communications has been either fired or "reassigned." His whereabouts are otherwise unknown. Ben Smith, writing for Politico, notes that Sergant was an "outsider from Washington's careful culture" -- that is, he was a novice in Washington's culture of stealth and subterfuge and did not absorb the culture quickly enough.

One cannot blame him for the gaucherie. Observe the hubris of Obama and the Democrats in how they propose their blatantly socialist legislation, thinly disguised in populist euphemisms. Why shouldn't Sergant have just emulated the tactics of the White House? But, he obviously had the cooperation or sanction of the White House to conduct the enlistment drive, perhaps with the sage guidance of White House staffer Marion Phillips, who, in an official blog post called "Facts are Stubborn Things" requested that "fishy" criticisms of the administration's plans for health care reform be reported to flag@whitehouse.gov.

Well, Courrielche had the decency to flag the White House and the NEA, instead. Nationally syndicated conservative columnist George Will also reported on the Big Hollywood exposé in "Artists in Harness" and in addition offers a brief critique of the NEA's anti-esthetic standards (without offering any standards of his own). These NEA beneficiaries, Will notes,

> "...are just another servile interest group seeking morsels from the federal banquet. Are they real artists? Sure, because in this egalitarian era, government reasons circularly: Art is whatever an artist says it is, and an artist is whoever produces art....For government today, 'art' is a classification so capacious it does not classify."

Bigger game to bring down than Yosi Sergant is Cass Sunstein, Obama's most recently appointed "czar," formally the administrator of the White House Office of Information and Regulatory Affairs, which is under the Office of Management and Budget, one of the few "czars" to be confirmed by the Senate. Sunstein, a tenured professor at the University of Chicago Law School, and who is married to Obama foreign policy adviser Samantha Power, began teaching at Harvard Law School in the fall of 2008. That didn't last long, because he is now on leave from Harvard to pursue the application of his collectivist theories and hypotheses.

Former dean of Harvard Law School and now U.S. Solicitor General Elena Kagan said of Sunstein on the announcement of his going to Harvard:

> "Cass Sunstein is the preeminent legal scholar of our time -- the most wide-ranging, the most prolific, the most cited, and the most influential. His work in any one of the fields he pursues -- administrative law and policy, constitutional law and theory, behavioral economics and law, environmental law, to name a non-exhaustive few -- would put him in the very front ranks of legal scholars; the combination is singular and breathtaking."

But, hoist Sunstein out of the swirling maelstrom of his interests, and you find a totalitarian, a "czar" in wolf's clothing. It is no coincidence that Obama, who was a mere "senior lecturer" at the University of Chicago Law School, would find him an appropriate choice to become a regulatory czar, one who can "regulate" just about everything he puts his mind to.

On environmentalism, he is open to persuasion. He argued against the so-called Precautionary Principle about the cost vs. benefit equation in enforcing environmental law, a position that raised the hackles of advocates of environmental crime and which he would be willing to reverse. He argues that animals should be represented in court. Apparently, he hasn't made up his mind about whether animals should be conveyed the attribute of "personhood" that would allow them to file lawsuits for abuse and cruelty.

Substitute the planet, the environment, and glaciers for animals, and Sunstein's reservations would fall like the Maginot Line. One can wonder why such a subject would fascinate Sunstein, but not for long. Individuals fare no better in his legalistic universe, in which ideas just hover in space and orbit no central philosophy.

On the First Amendment and freedom of speech, Sunstein has definite ideas. One of his "New Deals" would be a rewrite of the Constitution to allow for mandatory or compulsory "diversity" of views in virtually every medium of "public" communication, but most especially in television and on radio. In his book, *Democracy and the Problem of Free Speech* (1995), he argues that that such a rewrite would "reinvigorate the processes of democratic deliberation, by ensuring greater attention to public issues and greater diversity of views."

In order to attain that goal, which would be the resurrection of the Fairness Doctrine in all but name, he would support the creation of a federal panel of "nonpartisan experts" who would judge whether or not a television or radio station met their diversity criteria. If they did not, one imagines that they would refer the case and the offense to the Federal Communications Commission, which has the power to grant, deny or withdraw licenses to broadcast.

Sunstein proposes also that commercial broadcasters be required to subsidize "public" television or other commercial stations to ensure "less profitable but high-quality programming." All this regulating and requiring, he asserts, would not violate the "spirit" of the Constitution. One can presume that he doesn't regard the Sixteenth and Eighteenth Amendments as being in violation of that "spirit."

Again, one may wonder why he believes "diversity" is necessary. Clearly, the mainstream media are on the side of Obama and his plans to fit the nation for the yoke of servitude. Not even the anchors and shills of ABC, CBS and NBC could boast that 'diversity" thrives in the MSM. It is only

14

on "renegade" broadcasters such as Fox, and in conservative radio talk shows that "diversity" is not present, especially when they oppose the Obama and other collectivist agendas. One of Sunstein's interests, as noted above, is behavioral economics and law, which treats individuals as non-sentient atoms that coagulate into insulated groups, and, as atoms, autonomously make "decisions" that affect the marketplace and politics, and so, society.

This position meshes perfectly with his argument in his 2001 book, *Republic.com*, that the Internet is dangerous to "democracy" because on the Internet individuals may further choose to ally themselves with groups that reflect their values, and so repel the leveling influence of "diversity." This, argues Sunstein, permits individuals to reject information or positions that might challenge their beliefs. Ironclad convictions cannot be allowed. "Rational actors" should be gagged or banished to the fringe of "democracy." Open-mindedness should be made mandatory, even if it means regulating -- or censoring -- the Internet.

The object of that argument, of course, is not hard-core Democrats or wish-driven liberals, who, when faced with a rational argument against government-run health care, or smoking bans, or government-mandated nutrition guides, or public education, typically shut out reason in what Ayn Rand deemed "blanking out" the truth. In short, it is Sunstein's political friends and allies who insulate themselves from reason and rationality. If they choose not to think about individual rights, then they cannot exist.

In his 2004 book, *The Second Bill of Rights: FDR's Unfinished Revolution and Why We Need It More than Ever*, Sunstein advocates a "Second Bill of Rights," something proposed by Franklin D. Roosevelt in his State of the Union address in January, 1944. Like FDR's "four freedoms" (introduced in his address to Congress in 1941), these rights include rights to an education, to a home, to health care, and to protection against monopolies, all picked out of the space of floating abstractions.

How to pay for these rights? Taxation. Sunstein is tax happy. In an April 1999 Chicago Tribune Op-Ed he castigated tax "grumblers" on the advantages and virtues of taxation.

> "Without taxes there would be no property. Without taxes, few of us would have any assets worth defending....It may be reasonable, in some cases, to cut tax rates. What is unreasonable and, in fact, preposterous is the all-too-familiar conservative rhetoric that flatly opposes individual liberty to the government power to tax and

spend. You cannot be for rights and against government because rights are meaningless unless enforced by government…Rights to private property, freedom of speech, immunity from police abuse, contractual liberty, free exercise of religion--just as much as rights to Social Security, Medicare and food stamps--are taxpayer-funded and government-managed social services designed to improve collective and individual well-being…There is no liberty without dependency. That is why we should celebrate tax day. As Oliver Wendell Holmes, the great Supreme Court justice, liked to say, taxes are 'the price we pay for civilization.'"

Without taxes there would be no property? Which came first? The chicken or the egg? Has Sunstein ever imagined that the purpose of government is to *protect* rights -- *individual* rights, not community- or society- or government-bequeathed rights -- not to "enforce" them? Perhaps. If he had, he rejected the idea. Note that his idea of rights includes what could only be called government-created *entitlements*, such as Social Security, Medicare, and food stamps. If it can be argued that rights originate anywhere but in the nature of man as a being of volitional consciousness responsible for his own life and happiness, then, of course, these "rights" can be "enforced" by government. Therefore, the government owns the chicken and the egg, and the individual is merely a "steward" of property that somehow originates in government coercion acting for "society." Sunstein makes no distinction between them.

Sunstein's position was better articulated in an April 2005 blog entry in connection with a Yale University conference, "The Constitution in 2020," whose subject was the United States in the 21st century and how it should define itself. What should not be conceded at the conference, he suggested, was any notion that the Constitution should be regarded as an absolute defender of individual rights and liberty. An "absolutist" position on them is a natural enemy of "democratic deliberation." He warned that in debate:

I will be urging that it is important to resist, on the grounds of reason, the idea that the document should be interpreted to reflect the view of the extreme right-wing of the Republican Party. This idea, sometimes masquerading under the name of originalism or strict construction, represents a form of judicial hubris; it is bad history and bad law. It should be   exposed   and   rejected   as   such.

Sunstein's chief danger is his confessed ambition to be a *de facto* censor, or, as Ayn Rand characterized such a person in *Atlas Shrugged*, an intellectual cop. He would be perfect for the role. It is little wonder that

Obama nominated him for the office, given the president's own attempts to stifle freedom of speech and his wish for critics to not "do a lot of talking."

Cass Sunstein, for all his academic credentials and books, is just another member of the Chicago-Beltway wolf pack. Hear them yelp and howl for "democracy."

September 2009

Your Mild-Mannered Speech Therapist:
Cass Sunstein

Cass Sunstein, director of the Office of Information and Regulatory Affairs, will not like this column. He may be offended by it. Feel insulted. Cry "not fair!" He may recommend that I be taxed, or financially penalized somehow for expressing unapproved speech, or even incarcerated for having said such awful things about him. He endorses these ideas. Works assiduously for them. Has written extensively on how unbridled free speech imperils society and social stability, and so ought to be checked and even licensed.

So, sue me.

Well, he hasn't yet. In September 2009 I penned, "Cass Sunstein: 'Czar' in Wolf's Clothing," in which I excoriated him for sanctioning censorship and the manipulation of "public opinion" on the occasion of regiment of government arts-grantees being turned loose on the public by the National Endowment for the Arts. (I have written numerous articles on the perils facing the First Amendment and freedom of speech, including "'High Noon' for the First Amendment" in September 2009, which indict Sunstein, as well, including several articles for the *Journal of Information Ethics* and *The Encyclopedia of Library and Information Science.*)

Sunstein has published thirty-seven books to date, and a mountain of articles and papers. A man who has written so much may have a faulty memory and have difficulty remembering what he's written. On April 30th, for example, during a lecture at New York University Law School, an attendee asked him if he still endorsed an idea he proposed in a paper he wrote in 2008 while still fully employed at the University of Chicago Law School, "Conspiracy Theories" (before joining the faculty of Harvard Law School; Working Papers Nos. 08-3, 199, and 387).

In the question and answer portion of the lecture, *We Are Change* founder Luke Rudkowski confronted Sunstein concerning his avocation of a "provocateur" style program to silence what have become the government's most vociferous and influential critics.

With tongue firmly in cheek, Rudkowski introduced himself as "Bill de Berg from Brooklyn college," before directly asking Sunstein to explain his comments.

"I know you wrote many articles, but I think the most telling one about you is the 2008 one called 'Conspiracy Theories,' where you openly advocated government agents infiltrating activist groups for 9/11 truth, and also to stifle dissent online," Rudkowski stated.

"Why do you think the government should go after family members and responders who have questions about 9/11?" he asked Sunstein.

"I've written hundreds of articles and I remember some and not others," Sunstein replied, denying that he has a firm recollection of the paper.

"I hope I didn't say that, but whatever was said in that article, my role in government is to oversee federal rulemaking in a way that is wholly disconnected from the vast majority of my academic writing, including that," Sunstein added.

"I know that, I'm just asking because you may be the next Supreme Court Justice if Obama appoints you, and you did write those things," Rudkowski replied.

"I may agree with some of the things I have written but I'm not exactly sure. I focus on what my boss wants me to do," Sunstein said, intimating that he was just following orders.

When Rudkowski asked if Sunstein would retract his comments about banning opinions that differ from those of the government, Sunstein again claimed he did not remember the article he had written and his personnel intervened to prevent Rudkowski pressing him on the matter.

(I don't think Sunstein got the joke. Someone probably filled him in after the lecture. Rudkowski used as a pseudonym a play on The Bilderberg Conference – or Group or Club – an annual meeting in the Netherlands of influential Western politicians, businessmen, industrialists, and media heads. It is the subject of a conspiracy theory for world domination or world government, as have been the annual Pugwash Conference in Nova Scotia, the two-week Bohemian Club encampment in rural California, and the Council on Foreign Relations in New York City. There are also a number of private organizations the subject of conspiracy theories, such as the Masons and Yale University's Skull and Crossbones, among others. I employ some of these conspiracy theories in two of my novels, *The Daedâlus Conspiracy* and *Presence of Mind*, and not to the credit of the theories or their adherents.)

I have read all thirty pages of this paper. It is a ponderous, sociology-jargon riddled discourse that treats men as interchangeable, volitionless ciphers influenced by peer pressure, rumors, speculation and hearsay, as mere atoms of a social whole, the pawns and playthings of mysterious but unaccountable powers beyond their ken. Sunstein's paper is half Aldus Huxley's *Brave New World*, forty percent B.F. Skinner's *Beyond Freedom and Dignity*, and ten percent Orwell's *Nineteen Eighty Four*. His career position has been that the government has a natural adversarial interest and power to monitor, "manage," or otherwise counter men's thinking and speech it deems dangerous or potentially dangerous or disruptive.

That Sunstein could not remember having written this paper tests one's credulity. In it he expresses his central, fundamental political premises, one of which stands out: that the government has an obligation to oversee or police speech for the "greater good." Sunstein did not answer Rudkowski's question; he deftly pleaded advanced but selective Alzheimer's in the finest tradition of political stand-up evasion.

There is a sole thesis in "Conspiracy Theories": that the government should act to gag or confuse conspiracy theorists, which would include anyone with a plausible, credible theory of government malfeasance or inappropriate behavior, and not just wild-eyed, crackpot theories. Here are some choice statements from Sunstein's paper. He begins by citing all the conspiracy theories surrounding the 9/11 attacks, that they were either the work of the federal government or committed by terrorists with foreknowledge of them by the government. But then he diminishes his seriousness about the subject by deeming Santa Claus, the Easter Bunny and the Tooth Fairy as "conspiracy theories." Weeding through and enduring all the mushy verbiage about how and why conspiracy theories arise and gain currency, one is persuaded of one single thing about Sunstein's target: the safety and preservation of government power. Conspiracy theories jeopardize government, not the public. Conspiracy theories must be either spoken or recorded, and that action, regardless of the merits or lack of them of any given theory, comes under the protection of the First Amendment.

In Sunstein's worldview, the First Amendment is no guarantor of "democratic deliberation." It must be either rewritten, or complemented with legislation that will identify and regulate what the government deems as true and worthy of deliberation.

Which, of course, means censorship. Here are a sampling of excerpts from Sunstein's half-forgotten paper. The abstract sums up Sunstein's means and ends.

Those who subscribe to conspiracy theories may create serious risks, including risks of violence, and the existence of such theories raises significant challenges for policy and law. The first challenge is to understand the mechanisms by which conspiracy theories prosper; the second challenge is to understand how such theories might be undermined. Such theories typically spread as a result of identifiable cognitive blunders, operating in conjunction with informational and reputational influences.

A distinctive feature of conspiracy theories is their *self-sealing quality*. Conspiracy theorists are not likely to be persuaded by an attempt to dispel their theories; they may even characterize that very attempt as further proof of the conspiracy. Because those who hold conspiracy theories typically suffer from a "*crippled epistemology*," in accordance with which it is rational to hold such theories, the best response consists in *cognitive infiltration* of extremist groups. Various policy dilemmas, such as the question whether it is better for government to rebut conspiracy theories or to ignore them, are explored in this light. [*Italics* mine.]

Remember those italicized terms. They will come in handy later.

A further question about conspiracy theories – whether true or false, harmful or benign – is whether they are justified. Justification and truth are different issues; a true belief may be unjustified, and a justified belief may be untrue. (p. 6)

Confused yet? You may be justified in thinking that your car is powered by gas and internal combustion and electricity, but it may not be true. Sunstein will forgive you.

Karl Popper famously argued that conspiracy theories overlook the pervasive unintended consequences of political and social action; they assume that all consequences must have been intended by someone The basic idea is that many social effects, including large movements in the

21

economy, occur as a result of the acts and omissions of many people, none of whom intended to cause those effects. The Great Depression of the 1930s was not self-consciously engineered by anyone; increases in the unemployment or inflation rate, or in the price of gasoline, may reflect market pressures rather than intentional action. Nonetheless, there is a pervasive human tendency to think that effects are caused by intentional action, especially by those who stand to benefit (the *cui bono?* maxim), and for this reason conspiracy theories have considerable but unwarranted appeal. [p. 7]

Well, yes. Because natural phenomena are not the subject of the paper, all human action is attributable to intended consequences. Whether or not those consequences are intended to subjugate or mislead, or allow the actors to profit from them, is open to interpretation without evidence, but with evidence, those intentions can be proven. It is here, for the first of many times throughout his paper, that Sunstein implies that government policies that cause depressions, inflation, and gas prices, are excluded from any serious discussion of conspiracies. We can, however, determine motives from the consequences of those policies, such as the refusal of a government to allow oil exploration and drilling, or refusing to allow pipelines to be built, actions which result in higher gas prices. This is not rocket science or ethereal economics.

Sunstein continues to cite Popper:

> Popper captures an important feature of some conspiracy theories. Their appeal lies in the attribution of otherwise inexplicable events to intentional action, and to an unwillingness to accept the possibility that significant adverse consequences may be a product of invisible hand mechanisms (such as market forces or evolutionary pressures) or of simple chance, rather than of anyone's plans. A conspiracy theory posits that a social outcome evidences an underlying intentional order, overlooking the possibility that the outcome arises from either spontaneous *order or random forces.* [*Italics* mine, p. 7]

Random forces? Not a philosophy of altruism, not a system of collectivism? Ideas and ideologies play no role in Sunstein's explication of conspiracy theories. People just get all this foolishness in their heads.

> Members of informationally and socially isolated groups tend to display a kind of paranoid cognition and become increasingly distrustful or suspicious of the motives of others or of the larger

society, falling into a "sinister attribution error." This error occurs when people feel that they are under pervasive scrutiny, and hence they attribute personalistic motives to outsiders and overestimate the amount of attention they receive. Benign actions that happen to disadvantage the group are taken as purposeful plots, intended to harm. [p. 15]

That observation admirably describes how most of the American public is alienated from the Mainstream Media, which largely endorses and shills for harmful and intrusive government policies. There are a few independent news outlets that hove to true journalistic reporting. Fox News is one of them, so it is no wonder that some statists are demanding that the FCC revoke its broadcasting license. After all, reporting news of government corruption, policy failures, hypocrisy, and ignorance can be deemed a harmful "conspiracy theory," and we would all be better off without Fox News.

What can government do about conspiracy theories? Among the things it can do, what should it do? We can readily imagine a series of possible responses. (1) Government might ban conspiracy theorizing. (2) Government might impose some kind of tax, financial or otherwise, on those who disseminate such theories. (3) Government might itself engage in counterspeech, marshaling arguments to discredit conspiracy theories. (4) Government might formally hire credible private parties to engage in counterspeech. (5) Government might engage in informal communication with such parties, encouraging them to help. Each instrument has a distinctive set of potential effects, or costs and benefits, and each will have a place under imaginable conditions. However, our main policy idea is that government should engage in *cognitive infiltration* of the groups that produce conspiracy theories, which involves a mix of (3), (4) and (5). [*Italics* mine, p. 15]

Sunstein is comfortable with all these options, as he explains further on, although there are "cost and benefit" considerations to take into account. But, he would much prefer to play with the minds of Americans with "cognitive infiltration." Otherwise known as lies or half-lies.

Throughout, we assume a well-motivated government that aims to eliminate conspiracy theories, or draw their poison, if and only if social welfare is improved by doing so. (We do not offer a particular account of social welfare, taking the term instead as a placeholder for the right account.)

I think it is obvious which "social welfare" account Sunstein prefers – precisely the kind that exists now, a mixed economy which has grown less and less mixed under the current administration. Charging that administration with imposing a command, socialist economy on the country – after nearly four years of observation, evidence, and deduction --, would, in his parlance, be a "conspiracy theory" and come under the aegis of government action. Sunstein concludes his vaguely-recalled paper with:

> Some conspiracy theories create serious risks. They do not merely undermine democratic debate; in extreme cases, they create or fuel violence. If government can dispel such theories, it should do so. One problem is that its efforts might be counterproductive, because efforts to rebut conspiracy theories also legitimate them. We have suggested, however, that government can minimize this effect by rebutting more rather than fewer theories, by enlisting independent groups to supply rebuttals, and by cognitive infiltration designed to break up the crippled epistemology of conspiracy minded groups and informationally isolated social networks.

That call for more government power speaks for itself. But the public is no longer "informationally" isolated, or even starved. It has the Internet at its disposal to conduct its own judgment of what is true and what is false. Aside from the traditional repository of information, called books and libraries. And Sunstein has his beady eyes on the Internet to regulate it for the sake of ridding society of all those foolish ideas and theories, to better ensure that the public has the "truth."

And what, fundamentally, is a "conspiracy theory"? It is the contents of an individual's mind. And it is man's mind that Sunstein wishes the government to "infiltrate."

In May of 2010 The New York Times ran an adulatory, almost fawning appraisal of Sunstein and his policies, "Cass Sunstein Wants to Nudge Us."

> In "Nudge," a popular book that he wrote with the influential behavioral economist Richard Thaler, Sunstein elaborated a philosophy called "libertarian paternalism." Conservative

economists have long stressed that because people are rational, the best way for government to serve the public is to guarantee a fair market and to otherwise get out of the way. But in the real world, Sunstein and Thaler argue, people are subject to all sorts of biases and quirks. They also argue that this human quality, which some would call irrationality, can be predicted and — this is the controversial part — that if the social environment can be changed, people might be nudged into more rational behavior.

"Rational behavior" meaning obeying orders, and deferring to authority, especially government authority. Of course, Sunstein, Thaler and Benjamin Wallace Wells, author of the Times article, are also subject to all sorts of biases and quirks. The difference is that Sunstein in his present position wants to be able to enforce his biases and quirks. One shouldn't call that a "conspiracy," else one might find oneself burdened with a special "irresponsible speech" tax, or taken to court, or sent to a reeducation camp to have one's "crippled epistemology" cured by hard labor and epistemology-altering drugs.

Wells also confirms the existence of that paper Sunstein had difficulty remembering.

Sunstein had, during his academic career, a penchant for publishing trial balloons — they were a necessary part of his inquiry, a perpetual what if? Now, with their author a government official, some of these conjectures seem more worrisome. Sunstein has, for example, written often about the corrosive effects of rumors and falsehoods on democratic discourse (it is the subject of one of the two books that were published while he was waiting to be confirmed last year), and in a 2008 paper, he proposed that government agents "cognitively infiltrate" chat rooms and message boards to try to debunk conspiracy theories before they spread. The paper was narrowly concerned with terrorism, but to some, these were dark musings.

Dark musings or not, Wells approves. He needn't worry about having his thoughts "infiltrated." They've already been co-opted.

Let's take a look at what would be Cass Sunstein's interpretation of the American Revolution.

There were many American colonials who perceived a conspiracy by the Crown to enslave or indenture them to the Crown's benefit, or at least to the benefit of a handful of dissembling plotters.

Of course, from the Crown's perspective – and the Crown knew what was best for everyone, that was part of its job, its authority was the Book of All Knowledge – these dissatisfied and contentious colonials, most notably Patrick Henry, Thomas Jefferson, the Adams cousins, George Mason, and many others, all well-read in the political theories of John Locke and other antiquarian philosophers and theorists, and who were otherwise quite rational gentlemen, nonetheless were burdened with a "crippled epistemology" which inevitably skewed their perception of things. This epistemology permitted them to see dark designs where there were none in every action taken by the Crown, demonstrably taken for public order and the greater good.

These unfortunate gentlemen, who represented the "conspiracy entrepreneurs," rejected any and all explanations of Crown actions, and brooked no dissent within their own core membership. They tenaciously held onto their suspicion that the Crown was a semi-potent entity controlled by a small, secret clique in the deepest but most respectable recesses of the British establishment, who meant the colonies no good and sought to profit from the consequential misery of their distant charges.

In their dealings and correspondence between themselves, the colonials mutually reinforced their collective certainty of a conspiracy emanating from the most impenetrable bowels of the British government, and, in resisting all reasonable explanations, experienced an overwhelming and continuous "cascading" of consensual agreement concerning the means and ends of the Crown, even though some of them differed on specific points. All attempts by the Crown to "cognitively infiltrate" political discussions and gatherings and to sow seeds of discord, disinformation and misdirection, failed. The mechanisms of the conspiracy theorists were proof against tampering. The self-sealing "psychosis" of conspiracy proved too strong, and the Crown, otherwise unprepared to deal with such recalcitrant opposition to its benevolent policies, wondered if the best course of action might have been to simply ignore all colonials obsessed with their conspiracy theory. But, it was too late.

The conspiracy theorists finally took action. Their paranoia resulted in Jefferson's enumeration of libelous and slanderous (and, in other circumstances, actionable, they learned nothing from the John Wilkes affair) charges against the sovereign and his alleged lackeys in the Declaration of Independence. This curious document seemed to sanction any and all resistance to Crown authority, and served to deviously "objectify" their unfounded and delusional grievances against the Crown for the consideration of a "candid world" (neglecting the fact that most of it couldn't read anyway; the Declaration merely "preached to the choir").

This hysterical climax was preceded only a year before by an act of violence (predicted by a number of members of the Commons, notably Isaac Barré) committed by the lower ranks of subscribers to the conspiracy theory when they opposed with firearms a benign expedition by lawful authorities to find and destroy stockpiles of gunpowder and arms, which were intended by the conspiracy theorists to be used against the Crown without regard to law and order should it not belay its purported designs on the colonials. There was a tragic loss of life among those acting only to ensure the public's safety against "extremist" violence.

And we all know the consequences of this unfortunate episode of cognitive dissonance.

Except Cass Sunstein, your wannabe "speech therapist."

May 2012

A Renewed Assault on Freedom of Speech

House Minority leader Nancy Pelosi of California and her fellow Democrats wish to "amend" the First Amendment in order to prohibit corporations from saying anything or spending anything during national elections. There is some satisfaction to be had in no longer having to identify her as House Speaker. I never liked seeing her wield that gavel. Someone once remarked that a hammer in hand causes one to search for nails to pound in, and she was always searching for nails. She specialized in coffins.

It may be an act of desperation that moves her and her party to push for an "amendment" of the First Amendment in light of President Barack Obama's falling poll number -- numbers he seems determined to see fall every time he opens his mouth on any subject – to pull his reelection chances from the jaws of ignominious but well-deserved defeat. Or it may be an expression of defeat but an assurance that the Democrats will stick one more knife into America's back with such an "amendment," to better the party's chances of winning the White House in 2016 by loading the campaign   finance   dice.

Or it may be to establish a legacy of unprecedented malice and contempt for the country.

Think about it: It costs demagogues and wannabe totalitarians nothing to usurp the Constitution. They are all paid handsomely and enjoy fringe benefits and privileges most Americans could not afford. They are also exempt from having to submit to Obamacare. However, it will cost a concerned electorate time and money to combat and possibly see repealed or declared unconstitutional the blatant and sanctimonious thievery of our liberties and wealth. And that's only if the courts – especially the Supreme Court – is dealing with a full deck and understands the issues and what's at stake.

Or it may be an act of over-confidence that Obama will be reelected this November, regardless of his poll numbers, and here's a sample of what the Democrats plan to foist on the country after all the destructive "hope and change" of the last three and a half years. An amendment to the First Amendment would be no less a guarantee than how the Obamacrats fixed BHO's nomination and probable election in 2008 in several state caucuses and primaries with voter fraud and cooking the electoral books.

One really can't decipher what goes on inside the minuscule minds of Democrats, except that it's bound to be no good. That's for professional strategy watchers to second-guess.

Sporting what looked like a dry-cleaned Confederate Army officer's tunic, Pelosi explained why she wants to amend the First Amendment. She and her Democratic colleagues wish to prohibit corporations, regardless of their status as for-profits or non-profits, from having any role in political debate or in endorsing any candidate or idea. The Democrats harbor an unrelenting animosity for the *Citizens United v. Federal Election Commission* case of 2010, decided in favor of freedom of speech by the Supreme Court (at least partly; the whole 2002 Bipartisan Campaign Reform Act , a.k.a. the McCain–Feingold Act or "BCRA," ought to have been declared null and void). It weighs in the Democrats' collective political stomach like a helping of Yorkshire pudding, which often has the consistency of a lump of badly set cement.

Justice Anthony Kennedy, writing the majority 5-4 opinion, noted several key but not fundamental issues in *Citizens United.* Among them was that the First Amendment, expressing a broad principle that prohibits the government from discriminating between corporations and the news media, consequently, if only implicitly, prohibits the government from exempting newspapers, books, broadcast advocacy and blog sites from a law that suppresses the speech of individuals or entities not favored by the law. Newspapers, networks, and book and blog writers would have an unfair advantage over gagged corporations. To allow that power, would ultimately lead to the regulation or suppression of speech of the formerly exempted.

Kennedy also wrote that the broad protection of the principle behind the First Amendment applied to all individuals, either as persons or collectively in any association, such as a corporation, and that the government could not discriminate between individuals and associations. The identity of a "speaker" is irrelevant and should not carry an arbitrarily assigned stigma or prejudice against such associations. The fact that a group of individuals expressed a position on a candidate or an issue and happened to be expressing it under the aegis of a corporation, or spent money to express such a position or granted another entity (such as Citizens United) the funds to express that position, is irrelevant. The principle applies to all individuals, singly or in groups.

Corporations, the Court asserted, are groups of individuals, and the agreement of those individuals on specific issues, and the leave they grant

29

to a corporation to speak for them on those issues, should not prejudice such an arrangement. The First Amendment does not allow the government to impinge on the right of those individuals to express themselves in such a manner.

By extension, the Court applied the same arguments to the expenditure of money to speak freely in any manner.

The Court's finding was a "close analysis" of the issue – what I call "bean counting" – and not explicitly based on the principle of freedom of speech. It did not touch on the role of *property* as a means to exercise that freedom. Justice Clarence Thomas concurred with the majority opinion but wrote a rebuttal to it, saying that the whole campaign finance law should be stricken down, and not just that part of it that abridged on corporations' First Amendment rights.

Examine this exchange between Chief Justice John Roberts and the government attorney on the status of corporate money:

> In 2009, when the Supreme Court first heard oral arguments in the *Citizens United* case, Deputy Solicitor General Malcolm Stewart told the court that the administration believed the Constitution allowed the government to ban a corporation from using its general treasury funds to publish a book if the book advocated voting for something. "Take my hypothetical," Chief Justice John Roberts said to Stewart as he asked him about what kind of books the Obama administration believed it could constitutionally ban, "... This [book] is a discussion of the American political system, and at the end it says: Vote for X." "Yes," said Deputy Solicitor General Stewart, "our position would be that the corporation would be required to use PAC [political action committee] funds rather than general treasury funds." Roberts followed up: "And if they didn't, you could ban it?" "If they didn't, we could prohibit the publication of the book using corporate treasury funds," Stewart answered.

General treasury funds? Political action committee funds? Piggy bank funds? Money market funds? This is an example of bean-counting that eludes the Court, and Chief Justice Roberts did not or was not able to address the issue in terms of fundamentals. It shouldn't matter where the money comes from. It's private wealth being expended for private reasons.

Let us now turn to the perspective of that Wise Wasp Lady and former Speaker of the House. At the very beginning, she targets the Court's 2010 *Citizens United* finding.

> "We have a clear agenda in this regard: Disclose, reform the system reducing the role of money in campaigns, and amend the Constitution to rid it of this ability for special interests to use secret, unlimited, huge amounts of money flowing to campaigns," Pelosi said at her Thursday press briefing.

It's so unfair, isn't it? All those secret, unlimited, huge amounts of money flowing to campaigns. Which campaigns? Whose campaigns? Doubtless, Republican campaigns. The Democrats never did such a thing, don't you know? So this proposed abridgement of the First Amendment would not apply to the Democrats. Exempt from that abridgement would be People for the American Way, Media Matters, Common Cause, and any of George Soros's well-heeled front groups. They'll find a way around the amended Amendment and keep under wraps and out of sight, but it will be perfectly legal – until someone uncovers its illegality.

> "I think one of the presenters [at a Democratic forum on amending the Constitution] yesterday said that the Supreme Court had unleashed a predator that was oozing slime into the political system, and that, indeed, is not an exaggeration," said Pelosi. "Our Founders had an idea. It was called democracy. It said elections are determined by the people, the voice and the vote of the people, not by the bankrolls of the privileged few. This Supreme Court decision flies in the face of our Founders' vision and we want to reverse it."

It is difficult not to laugh at the first sentence. From the very beginning – nay, long before Obama set foot in the White House – the Democratic Party, with Obama as its iconic mover and shaker, has been responsible for a continuing flow of oozing and poisonous slime, such as TARP, Obamacare, the taxpayer-funded but failing "green" companies, the takeover of General Motors to reward and secure the unions, the creation of a kingdom of czardoms, cash-for-clunkers, the subsidy of various "artistic" groups to promote Obama's agenda, his opposition to making the country oil-independent of parasitical Mideast régimes, Fast & Furious, and an attempted court-packing with two individuals friendly to all

31

manner of collectivized rights, not individual rights. Among his other depredations, too numerous to list here.

Yes, Nancy, the Founders had an idea that escapes you. It wasn't "democracy" that they slaved to create, but a republican form of government whose Constitution specifically barred Congress and the Executive branch from infringing on individual rights. Built into that Constitution was a mechanism that would protect individuals from the mob rule of democracy. It says: the power of the people stops here. Not that Congress has been listening for the past century.

And you, Nancy, weren't clear on what exactly you want to reverse: the Founders' vision, or a Supreme Court decision that denies you the power to put corporations in government-mandated straight-jackets.

Pelosi was joined in her whimsical reflections on the Founders by two other enemies of the First Amendment.

> The participants noted that several members in both houses of Congress have offered various versions of an amendment to reverse Citizen United v. FEC and curb *unwanted speech* by corporations. Rep. Jim McGovern (D.-Mass.) is one of the members sponsoring an amendment. (*Italics* mine.)

> "I've introduced a People's Rights Amendment, which is very simple and straightforward," Rep. Jim McGovern (D.-Mass.) said at the forum. "It would make clear that all corporate entities, for-profit and non-profit alike, are not people with constitutional rights.

> "It treats all corporations, including incorporated unions and nonprofits, in the same way, as artificial creatures of the state that we, the people, govern, not the other way around," said McGovern.

Mr. McGovern is aptly named. No one ever said that corporations were "people." And note that he repeats that hoary old communist chestnut, that corporations govern and hold political power, and it oughtn't to be allowed. Notice also that their speech is "unwanted." *Unwanted* by whom? The "people"? Which "people"? Does Mr. McGovern include himself as one of those "people"?

No, corporations are not "creatures of the state." They are entities formed

32

for the protection of private property. Very likely McGovern would have advocated another old idea, that of granting all corporations "federal charters." Just as they did in Britain. Remember the East India Company? The royally chartered trading company whose tea was dumped into Boston Harbor? Americans fought a war against Britain for many reasons, and one of them was to get from under the powers and weight of "federally" chartered companies granted monopolies in trade.

Rep. Donna Edwards (D.-Md.) explained the basic principle this move to amend the Constitution is advancing.

> "In Citizens United, what the court said is that Congress has no authority to regulate this kind of political speech," said Edwards. "And so all of these constitutional amendments go to this question of giving Congress the authority that the Supreme Court, I think wrongly, decided isn't within Congress's constitutional--our constitutional purview.

> "And so, you know, the traditional rights of free speech that we have known as citizens would not be disturbed by any of these constitutional amendments," said Edwards. "But what it would do is it would say, all of the speech in which, whether it's corporations or campaign committees and others engage in, would be able to be fully regulated under the authority of the Congress and--and under our Constitution."

> "I mean, in my view, a corporation is not a person. It is not an individual," said Edwards. "The rights that it has are those that are granted by the state, granted by the, by the Congress."

Donna Edwards doesn't seem certain what she is saying. Bluntness is not her style. She dances around the idea that Congress or a delegated committee of empowered interlopers, such as the Federal Election Commission, should regulate speech. Well, what would Congress or the FEC allow a corporation to say? Would it depend on how much money the corporation was willing to spend? Or would it depend on whether or not Congress or the FEC agreed with what the corporation wished to say? This idea is as fuzzy in her head as it is in the other forum heads.

She does repeat a fallacy subscribed to by both Democrats and Republicans: that freedom of speech is "traditional." No, it isn't traditional. It isn't a ritual or practice whose origins are lost in the mists of time, something to be updated or discarded or preserved because it's old fashioned or because it's been done over seven score generations. Freedom of speech is integral to the individual in society. If a man must speak out in favor of justice or to defend his life and property, he must be able to speak without hindrance or obstruction, provided it is by means of his property or that of another individual or a corporation.

But the campaign finance law already regulates the property – that is, the money – which is an issue that has not been addressed by the Supreme Court, at least it wasn't in *Citizens United*. Pelosi's forum wishes to close that limited route of expression entirely.

The Founders denied Congress the authority to prohibit speech for any reason. Nevertheless, Pelosi et al. want it for specious reasons, one of them being that Democrats don't wish to have to compete in the realm of political   persuasion.

This is the leitmotif of ambitious, not-yet-ready-for-prime-time tyrants. Nancy Pelosi, of course, would like the amendment to the First Amendment hammered out behind closed doors, and once it's passed the House and the Senate and is on its way to the Oval Office. Then we can see   what's   in   it.

Censorship for some, for now. Followed inexorably by censorship for all, forever.

April 2012

The Vilification of Freedom of Speech

Slate joined the tut-tut mob of dhimmified American pundits and commentators by endorsing the abridgement of the First Amendment, at the behest of thin-skinned, super-sensitive Muslims, in its September 25th article, "The Vile Anti-Muslim Video Shows That the U.S. Overvalues Free Speech."

Slate is proof that the Internet isn't wholly a refuge from the Mainstream Media. It has its complement of liberal, leftist and myopic sites that range from banal to bizarre to outlandishly vitriolic. It isn't immediately apparent in the Slate article, written by Editor Eric Posner, that it denigrates not only the First Amendment, but anyone upholding its sanctity, because it took him ten paragraphs of irrelevant commentary to reach the conclusion that the First Amendment is ready for a tweaking and perhaps even a rewrite that would favor Muslims and Islam.

Robert Spencer zeroed in on the key statement in the *Slate* article in his Jihad Watch article of September 26th, and dismisses it with brevity. He quotes from *Slate* first:

> "That's because the First Amendment protects verbal attacks on groups as well as speech that causes violence (except direct incitement: the old cry of "Fire!" in a crowded theater). And so combining the liberal view that government should not interfere with political discourse, and the conservative view that government should not interfere with commerce, we end up with the bizarre principle that **U.S. foreign policy interests cannot justify any restrictions on speech whatsoever. Instead, only the profit-maximizing interests of a private American corporation can. Try explaining that to the protesters in Cairo or Islamabad."** (**Bold** emphasis is Spencer's)

Spencer: "In other words, surrender before they hit us again."

That's all that need be said.

Spencer handily runs other publication over the coals in his Jihad Watch/Atlas Shrugs article, "The Suicide of the Free Press," on how and why other publications are picketing against the First Amendment. Citing the example of the *Los Angeles Times'* Op-Ed by Sarah Chayes, a career do-gooder currently with the Carnegie Endowment for International Peace, Spencer asks:

> But the larger question is, why is the Los Angeles Times coming down on the side of restrictions on the freedom of speech in the first place? Are they not aware that such restrictions, if implemented, can and probably will be used against them? While the Los Angeles Times editors are no doubt serene in their certainty that they will never print anything that will insult Islam or Muslims, there could all too easily come a time when a governing authority deems something they have published to be "hateful" or even"deliberately tailored to put lives and property at immediate risk," and – if free speech by then has been restricted – that will be the end of the Times as an outpost of the free press.

Further, there is Posner's "profit-maximizing" qualifier coupled with the "interests of a private American corporation" that reveals *Slate*'s anti-capitalist leanings. We'll leave that alone for the time being, although it would be interesting to know why Posner thought it necessary to say that and not something to the effect, "Only the speech of private individuals can be restricted or interfered with in political discourse," because it boils down to the same thing: restrictions *à la carte*. And what has "commerce" to do with the issue? I don't think Posner agrees with Ayn Rand that freedom of speech is dependent on the status of private property. So, one can only scratch one's head in trying to comprehend the legal universe Posner occupies and speaks from.

President Barack Obama said at the U.N. that "The future must not belong to those who slander the prophet of Islam."

Or criticize him? Or resort to Charlie Hebdo level cartoons? Or to awful video trailers whose Muslim funding is just now coming to light? (See Walid Shoebat's revelations here; apparently the "Innocence of Muslims" has a not-so-innocent pedigree.) One might be tempted to say, "Nor should the future belong to those who slander Jesus. Or Ayn Rand. Or any one of H.L. Mencken's dead gods." But that would be conceding the premise that speech about these figures ought to be "restricted."

Sorry, old chap, but the future belongs to me, a slanderer, mocker, blasphemer, and critic of Muslims and Islam and its pedophilic icon, Big Mo. What's the government going to do about it? Ask Huma Abedin to send some ski-masked jihadist thugs to beat me up? Give me the Daniel Pearl treatment? Or perhaps Secretary of State Hillary Clinton will request that a joint DHS/TSA Swat team swoop down on me and take me in for questioning.

Posner opined that Obama's speech contained "a strong defense of the First Amendment." In fact, it was one of the most tepid but insidious "defenses" of an American freedom on record. Why? Posner is a professor at the University of Chicago Law School. He ought to have noted the *quid pro quo* which Obama had no business offering the United Nations, the OIC, the world that doesn't like our First Amendment, and Muslims: You stop slandering Jesus, we'll stop slandering Mohammad.

That's tantamount to agreeing to give the school yard bully your money and your lunch, and he agrees to stop giving you a black eye and dunking your head in a commode.

Muslims won't stop slandering other creeds' icons – try and stop them– but how does Posner propose to stop the slandering, libeling, or mockery of Mohammad, except by applauding the criminalization of speech at the behest of the Organization of Islamic Cooperation, the United Nations, Hillary Clinton, and anyone else who doesn't like the First Amendment?

The criminalization of speech about Islam is a proposed exercise in people management and Platonic guardianship by elitists ensconced in the ivory tower of indemnified statism. It is supposed to combat violence and bridge the gap between Western and Islamic civilizations. But Islam isn't a "civilization"; it is an ideology hell-bent on conquest. But as Daniel Greenfield points out in his essay, "Muslim Multiculturalism and Western Post-Nationalism" notes:

> The left's post-national identity is based on a secular political multiculturalism. Islam's post-national identity is based on a religious theocratic multiculturalism. The left has heresies that it prosecutes as hate crimes and Islam has heresies that it prosecutes as blasphemy.

> Progressives have been always too stupid to understand that the consequences of their progressivism in undermining the current, more advanced, phase of human society is the restoration of reactionary social and political systems. In Russia, the Bolsheviks toppled an intermediary government and restored a Czar named Stalin and feudalism under the name of collectivism, to the proud cheers of the world's leftists at the progress they were making. In the Arab Spring, they brought back Islamism and they have

brought it back in London and Sydney, and Paris and New York as well.

My advice to Eric Posner: Think about what you're asking for. You just might have your way. But, you may regret your not being able to say what you wish to say about anything. Criminalizing speech about Islam doubtless will set a poison pill precedent to criminalize speech about *anything* the state deems protected, sacrosanct, and not open to discussion.

You may someday need to shout "Fire!" and won't, because you've surrendered your right to. To you, it won't seem practical. Or right. You've "progressed" to a more "mature" standard of speech. Besides, it would be against the law. Shouting "Fire!" might provoke someone to throw a Molotov cocktail.

You would be hard-pressed to prove to the authorities that it wasn't your intention to provoke the thrower of the Molotov cocktail. You would protest: That was *his* action, not yours. You were merely trying to save lives. He was trying to take lives. How awful! Still, your action "triggered" his action.

You would be held responsible. The law would say so. Hands behind your back, please. These are plastic cuffs, and won't hurt a bit.

September 2012

ABC News a.k.a. OBC News

The Drudge Report was the first to announce the latest step in the fascist/socialist march to dictatorship in the United States. To guarantee that there is no "debate" on the government's plan to impose mandatory health care "reform" on the nation, President Barack Obama has made a deal with ABC News to conduct a phony prime time "town hall" style meeting from the Blue Room of the White House on June 24. The sanctimonious and overly chummy anchor Charles Gibson will host "World News" from that precious vantage point. He will welcome the nation to the to the first airing of the Obama Broadcasting Corporation.

Not even FDR was brazen enough to co-opt a broadcaster to shill for the New Deal.

No one in the Reichstag -- excuse me, in Congress -- is protesting this blatantly bogus "reality show" except in the most wimpish manner. Republican National Committee chief of staff Ken McKay, according to Drudge, "fired off a complaint to the head of ABC News." The text of his letter is really just a complaint that the Republicans have not been invited to participate in the "debate."

> "Today, the RNC requested an opportunity to add our Party's views to those of the President's to ensure that all sides of the health care reform debate are presented. Our request was rejected."

Drudge reported that ABC News Senior Vice President Kerry Smith replied to the RNC, claiming it contained "false premises."

> "ABC News prides itself on covering all sides of important issues and asking direct questions of all newsmakers -- of all political persuasions -- even when others have taken a more partisan approach and even in the face of criticism from extremes on both ends of the political spectrum. ABC News is looking for the most thoughtful and diverse voices on this issue. ABC News alone will select those who will be in the audience asking questions of the president....ABC News will have complete editorial control. To suggest otherwise is quite unfair to both our journalists and our audience."

Kerry Smith's rebuttal must be taken with a hefty dose of sea salt. She is as much a liar as Obama when he states he doesn't want to run a car company, or the banking industry, or any American business. "Thoughtful and diverse voices" are the last thing she and Obama want to hear. Note the disparagement of any political opposition that is to be excluded as a "partisan approach," and the dismissal of "criticism from extremes on both ends of the political spectrum" as a kind of unnecessarily divisive "polarization." There is no such thing as an objectively verifiable truth, according to Smith, just a comfortable, non-judgmental middle ground amenable to the wishes of an administration willing to initiate force in its quest to "do good."

Given the leftist bias of ABC News (and of its rivals, CBS and NBC), one can guess the composition of the audience and predict the kinds of prearranged questions that will be asked Obama. Sure, ABC News will "select" the audience and have "complete editorial control," but not without every person and virtually every word first being vetted by chief of staff Rahm Emanuel and press secretary Robert Gibbs and whoever else on Obama's staff is responsible for scripts.

This kind of circus will not be put on without an enormous amount of preparation, and every precaution will be taken to prevent any untoward "dialogue" between Obama and any of the dupes in the audience. The June 24th broadcast will have all the spontaneity of a White House press conference. Furthermore, ABC News has always broadcast from one extreme end of the political spectrum, that of total government control over everything. It is immaterial, however, which network was chosen to be Obama's stalking horse. They are all equally culpable.

The denial for "equal time" should have come as no surprise. The Republicans, because they abandoned individual rights and reason, can only suggest a watered-down version of socialized health care. They will not oppose the idea of socialized medicine. Why should Obama and Congress settle for less when they have demonstrated they can go the limit with no fundamental opposition?

Did ABC deny the request? Yes. On its own initiative? Doubtful. Neither Obama nor his allies in Congress want to hear any other "views" on socialized medicine. Therefore, any request for "equal time" is unwelcome. Rational arguments against socialized medicine and health care would only prove to be distractions, or worse, illuminating. The arrangement is a preview of the reinstatement of the "Fairness Doctrine" under another label, a doctrine whose very nature guarantees the suppression of dissent for as long as the government controls the airwaves and has the power to dictate the content and character of speech. Obama and the Democrats want to enact that doctrine without it being called censorship. If ABC wishes to continue to be the favored network, it will take orders. Apparently, that will be voluntarily.

There must be more behind ABC's anointment than just a "deal." One can imagine the bidding war for Obama's favor between ABC, CBS and NBC; one cannot help but wonder what promises ABC made to the White House for this show and for all future "town halls." One can even speculate on the reasons behind the choice of Gibson as the "moderator" of the forthcoming broadcast. CBS anchor Katie Couric has little or no verisimilitude. Anchor Brian Williams of NBC is even more abrasively sanctimonious and authoritarian than is Gibson. One can only suppose it was decided that Gibson's features are less annoying and patronizing. Image is everything. They don't want to bore or frighten the kiddies.

Drudge reports that the arrangement has "ignited an ethical firestorm." But this development represents more than an issue of ethics. It represents a paucity of moral courage, which I do not believe ABC News ever knew the meaning of or was ever bothered by, coupled with a blind avarice for high ratings. Most importantly, ABC News endorses the government's rapidly expanding control of not only the economy but of virtually every aspect of the lives of this country's citizens. But the fact remains that all three news anchors and their co-anchors report the government's wishes as the metaphysically given. "It is raining outside." "You will be fined by the government for not enrolling in its health care program." Period.

The print press is no less guilty. Frank Rich, for example, in his New York Times article of June 14, "The Obama Haters' Silent Enablers," was moved to smear any verbal opposition to the Obama agenda as goading "violent extremists." This position is in complete agreement with the DHS memo of April (discussed in "A Cavalcade of Collectivism," April 17), which lumped together all opposition, rational, semi-rational and irrational, as phenomena to be monitored and possibly stymied by the authorities, and insinuates that it is this kind of "free speech" that provokes assassins and civil unrest. To judge by the frenetic tone of his op-ed, Rich would likely welcome an Obama and Congressional version of Hitler's 1933 Enabling Act, one that would suppress all "provocative" speech.

One cannot doubt the news media's complicity in bringing fascism to this country. It is a complicity whose root is not some vast ignorance of what was being done. Ignorance of the law of identity is no excuse for breaking it; in an individual, reality will correct such ignorance. But there is no possible excuse, either, for a news organization that poses as politically sophisticated. It acts with full knowledge of the fraud and deception perpetrated by the Democrats on the country ever since Obama announced his candidacy for the presidency.

The accession of ABC News as a *de facto* department of the Obama administration ought to serve as convincing evidence of that complicity.

June 2009

Politics

A Brief Aside on Power

In my May 7th commentary, "'Civility' per Obama," I noted that:

> One can't question someone's views or positions without delving into his motives and patriotism. (e.g., "Sir, if you know the idea is patently fraudulent, stupid, and costly, why are you *for it?*") (Emphasis mine)

I would like to briefly expand on that comment, for it is important to understand the motivation of those responsible for what can only become a catastrophe for this country. It is important for Americans to grasp it, whether they are for or against ObamaCare or any other law this administration in particular authors and imposes on the country. It is crucial that men understand what moves those who advocate the blatantly demonstrable irrational. If more Americans understood it, perhaps the allure of state-managed existence in any realm would diminish and vanish, and its advocates and supporters be exposed for the monsters they are.

I characterized the words, actions, and attitude of President Barack Obama, Nancy Pelosi, Harry Reid, and others in Washington, concerning their desire to have ObamaCare and other statist legislation passed and enacted as law, in resolute disregard for individual rights, Constitutional limitations on executive and Congressional power, and of the proven opposition to their ends, as *scabrous arrogance*. It is why they are "for it" in the face of all the evidence, available to anyone, that their legislation can only lead to destruction, misery, and impoverishment.

The key to such legislation is the role of compulsion, or force. The arrogance is rooted in the power to compel one to act against one's values, against one's own life. The monsters wish to truly GOVERN people, not let them alone. In the past I have criticized the sloppy and dangerous usage of the terms *govern* and *democracy*, and will not repeat myself here. But, free men have no need of the monsters. Men who agree that they should be "governed" or "ruled" by them are of no interest to them, either. Novelist-philosopher Ayn Rand wrote in her 1941 pamphlet, "To All Innocent Fifth Columnists"

> *The Totalitarians do not want your active support.* They do not need it. They have their small, compact, well-organized minority, and it is sufficient to carry out their aims. And they want from you is your indifference.

And one's indifference can complement the indifference of the legislators. Such indifference, as Rand explains, is a silent sanction of their actions and policies.

But free, independent men are truly hated by our "leaders," who are power-lusters first class. "Governing" otherwise free men -- making them think and act in ways free men might not otherwise think or act -- is their chief and principal end. If the element of compulsion or force were not woven into their laws, they would have no interest in such legislation -- they would have no reason to act, no reason to seek office, no reason to persuade their future serfs and slaves that it is in their best interests to become serfs and slaves.

Ellsworth Toohey, in *The Fountainhead*, in answer to Peter Keating's question of why Toohey wanted to kill the hero, Howard Roark, answered:

> "I don't want to kill him. I want him in jail. You understand? In jail. In a cell. Behind bars. Locked, stopped, strapped -- and alive. He'll get up when they tell him to. He'll eat what they give him. He'll move when he's told to move, and stop when he's told. He'll walk to the jute mill, when he's told, and he'll work as he's told. They'll push him, if he doesn't move fast enough, and they'll slap his face when they feel like it, and they'll beat him with rubber hose if he doesn't obey. And he'll obey. He'll take orders. *He'll take orders!*"*

That is the fundamental, base, evil motivation of those who wish to employ force, dramatized and expressed by Toohey, who relishes the prospect of seeing Roark -- or anyone like him -- in fetters and not free to live his own life.

You will take orders. You will be locked, stopped, and strapped, and you'll do as you're told if you wish to stay alive, whether you are a complacent altruist or intransigent individualist. You will obey, else you will go to jail -- or live in a country that has been transformed into a jail; that is the true meaning of Obama's slogan, "hope and change," all of his "audacious" policies and appointments and laws are geared to that aim -- or see your bank accounts cleaned out by the government, or your house seized by it, or your wages garnisheed at the whim of an anonymous bureaucrat.

You will help Obama, Pelosi, Reid *et al.* make their "ideal" society work, even though they know, but do not tell you, that jails and prisons of whatever size -- whether it is a county jail or a federal prison or a whole country -- are not independent, self-sustaining organizations, which must collapse because production is not their purpose. Witness the campaign of conquest of the Nazis when they became a fully-empowered totalitarians. Their purpose is to contain and control -- and to exact *obedience* from its inmates, regardless of their willingness or recalcitrance, regardless of their economic status or profession, regardless of the expected consequences, which is destruction. For a dramatization of those consequences, see Rand's *Atlas Shrugged.*

That is the long and short of the motivation behind those who would "govern" Americans. It is as important an issue to understand as the fallacy and evil underlying any collectivist system. That motivation is intimately and inexorably linked to the idea of force.

*Ayn Rand, *The Fountainhead* (1943). New York: Penguin/Plume Centennial Edition, 2005, p. 663.

May 2010

The Bedlam of Statism

Is statism bipolar? Schizophrenic? Autistic? Obsessive-compulsive? Multi-phobic? Inherently dysfunctional? Psychotically antisocial? A form of dementia? A narcissistic personality disorder? A kind of panic or anxiety disorder? Just plain maladaptive? Or all of the preceding? This column will enter the mad house of statism and explore its various wards.

John David Lewis, in his masterpiece about the means and ends of war, *Nothing Less Than Victory*, cites both Ludwig von MIses and Ayn Rand on *etatism* and *statism* or *fascism.*

> In *Omnipotent Government*, von Mises notes that *etatism* denotes those political systems that "have a common goal of subordinating the individual unconditionally to the state, the social apparatus of compulsion and coercion." (Lewis, p. 44)

Quoting from Rand's column, "The Fascist New Frontier," Lewis cites Rand:

> The dictionary definition of fascism is: "a governmental system with strong centralized power, permitting no opposition or criticism, controlling all affairs of the nation (industrial, commercial, etc.), emphasizing an aggressive nationalism . . ." [*The American College Dictionary*, New York: Random House, 1957.]

Of statism, she also wrote:

> If the term "statism" designates concentration of power in the state at the expense of individual liberty, then Nazism in politics was a form of statism. In principle, it did not represent a new approach to government; it was a continuation of the political absolutism— the absolute monarchies, the oligarchies, the theocracies, the random tyrannies—which has characterized most of human history.

Lewis continues:

> Statism applies to any government with such power, whether a primitive tribal ruler, a theocratic council, or a communist or fascist dictatorship – including a democracy unrestrained by

fundamental laws – each of which swallows the lives and fortunes of individuals without regard for their rights. The identification of such governments as statist is relatively new, but the practice is of enormous antiquity (as Lewis demonstrates in his chapter on the Theban Wars against the Spartan slave state).

But the subject here is that wherever statism in any of its forms has been established and tried, it has failed, causing economic dislocations and eventual collapse, the impoverishment of its most productive citizenry, their incremental or outright slavery, and an excuse to war on more prosperous and freer neighbors. The history of statism is riddled with these disasters, and at no time has it ever been successful on its own terms, nor will it ever be. Even with a willing and compliant citizenry, it is destined to fail.

If Nazi Germany and Soviet Russia seemed to be "successful," it was only by grace of the inertia of the semi-free past and a proximity to freer nations, which they immediately began to conquer. The longevity of statism is illusory. Today mixed economies are endemic and seem to thrive only because of the shrinking quantum of liberty and capitalism that may exist in any one nation, and on which statist governments depend for revenue (or loot). Governments produce nothing, not even the desks and chairs and pencils and grosses of paper and ink used by bureaucratic chiefs and their staffs.

Remember that even in the U.S., there are no such things as government-owned and run gun or tank factories, only private companies contracted to produce weaponry or the instruments of force (such as Tasers, electronic cattle prods, protective gear, etc.). The only government-owned and managed "enterprises" by tyrannies have been the charnel houses of concentration camps and Gulags. The exceptions to this rule are communist nations in which the government owns and runs everything and everyone. Even in such overtly totalitarian countries, however, their governments are thieves and parasites preying on the achievements of freer nations. The phenomenon has been amply recorded by many observers, such as Werner Keller and Anthony C. Sutton.

Look at Saudi Arabia, or Venezuela, or "capitalist" China: these are countries that thrive on the products of freedom, while outlawing it for their own populaces. And their longevity is sustained only by the ignorance of those who help them survive, such as Western policymakers, pragmatic businessmen, and tourists.

So, if statism, whatever its form or scope, has a consistent record of tragic and costly failure whenever and wherever it has been tried, what is its appeal? Why do men keep advocating it and imposing it in the face of the incalculable destruction, death and misery it has caused?

It must be madness. A form of mental illness in politicians, leaders, and their followers. It's easier to champion than are rational self interest, individualism, and no-strings-no-fetters freedom. Collectivism appeals to politicians because it guarantees votes and power. It appeals to voters because it proposes to share the misery of having one's wealth and that of one's neighbor expropriated for the greater good of an anonymous, amorphous whole, that omnivorous monster called "society." The joke is that sacrificing for the "greater good" is not a virtue, but a vice resting on delusions, obsessions, unreasoning malice, or unexamined fears.

Altruism, the morality that underlies collectivism and statism, is a form of madness. It asks a person to value ice cream by never tasting it, or to sacrifice it after one has tasted it. It asks one to value life by not living. It demands that one surrender one's liberty in exchange for an entitlement. It requires that one not *know* that one's rights and freedom originate in the requirements of living as an independent individual, but to *believe* that one's rights originate with society or the state to be granted or withdrawn when the state deems it politick.

Daniel Greenfield made this observation:

> The Clash of Civilizations is all-encompassing. It doesn't just cover the big thing, like ramming planes into skyscrapers, but also the little things…. For Mayor Bloomberg, it's banning large sodas….When there is no limit to government infringement on rights, then the law is a collection of bugbears and control mechanisms…. It's senseless, but so is fighting obesity by banning people from buying large sodas. When the obsession of a few men is turned into law, then the result is equally contemptuous of the individual as a rotting sack of vile habits which he has to be forced to abandon by the majority of the law.
>
> Once you abandon the rights of the individual to the fiat of activists, judges and politicians-- then laws can be made by anyone who wants them badly enough. The same process of judicial activism, hysteria, violent attacks, and pressure groups that created gay marriage can one day lock up the happy couples. It's only a matter of who is making the laws.

Statism is legalized, institutional irrationality, criminality elevated to the status of duty and "public service." The irrational, by itself, operating in a social vacuum, is self-destructive. Operating unchecked or unchallenged among men, is destructive of them and of their values.

Walter Williams, in his article, "Immoral Beyond Redemption," poses the question:

> ...[D]oes an act that's clearly immoral and illegal when done privately become moral when it is done legally and collectively? Put another way, does legality establish morality? Before you answer, keep in mind that slavery was legal; apartheid was legal; the Nazis' Nuremberg Laws were legal; and the Stalinist and Maoist purges were legal. Legality alone cannot be the guide for moral people. The moral question is whether it's right to take what belongs to one person to give to another to whom it does not belong.

From science fiction, statism can be characterized by a variety of malevolent, inimical creatures. In our public education systems (including universities), children and young people are mandated to sit in front of *Alien* pod teachers from which leap parasites that cling fast to their minds to plant the seeds of multiculturalism, volunteerism, self-sacrifice, and deference to the state. In economics, we are all attacked by *The Blob* of taxes, controls, and prohibitions that eat us alive. *Predators* identify and hunt down anyone who defends himself word or deed against government force.

From the horror genre, the intelligentsia and its cohorts in academe may be represented by *Hannibal Lecter*, a charming, articulate killer who will promise men the moon while plotting to prepare a meal of them for himself.

Let's say that statism is bipolar. A bipolar government takes action, such as imposing confiscatory taxes that skew, reduce, or redirect private spending for the sake of raising revenue to support sometimes legitimate but too often illegitimate imperatives and programs. The decades-old campaign against smoking is salutary. Politicians, heeding the demands of anti-smoking lobbies and activists, impose higher taxes and more controls on cigarettes and other tobacco products, theoretically reducing smoking rates among the population (a state-designated "public good"), and allowing anti-smokers and the asthma-stricken and sensitivity feigners to frolic in businesses, restaurants, and bars they don't really own.

At the same time, however, government depends on cigarette taxes for revenue, and when the revenue falls, it raises the taxes on cigarettes higher, or finds another taxable product – say, gasoline, or capital gains, or bottles of imported Bailey's Irish Cream – to make up for a shortfall that becomes increasingly bottomless. (And incidentally creates an "illegal" or underground market for the targeted goods, from smuggled, untaxed cigarettes to outlawed light bulbs to profits deposited in offshore banks, which in turn causes to the government to create more agencies and hire more employees to "police" said market, which in turn requires more taxes and revenue to pay for enforcement.)

A statist or command economy is therefore a Sisyphean nightmare that grows worse with each new echelon of salaried mediocrities put in charge of regulating the latest "public concern." Statists declare society blighted and proceed to impose eminent domain on neighborhoods, choices, habits, and everyone. This has been the incremental history of Progressivism, which has never had to look far for a "social ill" to cure and regulate. Any human action may be deemed a "social ill" and a candidate for taxation, regulation, or prohibition, from consuming milkshakes to stock or commodity speculation.

The purpose of the taxes, regulations, and prohibitions is to impose the "social justice" clamored for by various social engineering groups that wish to punish, control, or extinguish other groups. Governments – federal, state and local – wish to have enough revenue to either balance their budgets, or at least stave off bigger than usual deficits, while at the same time heeding the social justice brigades' demands for smoke-free air or reduced car emissions or nutritional information on food products or a "fairer" redistribution of earned income. This compels government policymakers to seek a median, which only ratchets up costs all around. It is a no-win episode of bipolarism for everyone, two steps forward, one step back. It is disguised as "social progress" by the pronouncements of activists, politicians, and public interest groups. What it is in reality is an insidious conditioning of men so that they become inured to slavery.

Some of those activists, politicians, and public interest groups know exactly what it is all progressing to – socialism, fascism, a straightjacket state – but most don't know, and think that once the tax, regulation, or prohibition is legislated, their work is done. They've done their good deed, and remain on the sidelines or become spectators while other activists, politicians, and public interest groups take their turn at "democracy."

It is all a prescription for bedlam, of groups fighting each other for controls over each other, a "democratic" anarchy that can only result in the stasis of totalitarian rule.

Choose your dementia from the group of statist disorders which introduced this column. As with personal, clinically defined mental illnesses, each is founded on some species of the irrational.

When are Americans going to stop believing in the miracle nostrums of statism, and seek out and heed the advice of those who prescribe the steps to take toward the sanity of freedom?

June 2012

Kid Care:

The Trojan Horse of Socialized Medicine

"It's a sideshow of a sideshow," complained the British general in Cairo at the beginning of David Lean's *Lawrence of Arabia*, describing the campaign against the Turks and Germans in the Mideast during World War I. As history notes, the resolution of that sideshow by Western powers spawned greater problems for them in later decades, with the British and French creating the artificial regimes of Jordan, Syria, Lebanon and Iraq.

Kuwait had been a British protectorate since 1899, while Saudi Arabia is a consequence of Wahhabist campaigns of conquest since the 18th century. The seven members of the United Arab Emirates were also sired by Western political expediency.

Of course, these are all Islamic countries, and some have gone beyond looking the gift horse in the mouth by either demanding submission of the West or calling for its defeat and eradication. Others, such as the UAE are too busy fleecing the West in enormous and extortionate wealth transfers via petrodollars to bother with a jihadist campaign of conquest, though there is plenty of evidence they are passive enablers of it.

The "sideshow" discussed here is an action of Congress that would greatly expand the welfare state. According to a *Los Angeles Times* article of October 7:

> "President says he'd compromise on insurance," the congressional bill "would spend $60 billion over five years to expand health coverage for children of the working poor and middle-class, and it would pay for it with higher tobacco taxes."

The article reports that President Bush's "long-promised veto Wednesday set off an ideological battle about who holds responsibility for extending health-care benefits to uninsured children: the government or the private sector.

"Bush has offered $30 billion, a 20 percent increase over current levels but not enough to maintain the existing enrollment in what is known as the State Children's Health Insurance Program [SCHIP], budget analysts say.

52

"The program is managed by states within federal guidelines and serves about 6 million children. An estimated 9 million children remain uninsured in the U.S., and the number has been rising as employers cut back coverages."

Let's subject this reporting to some rational analysis.

The "ideological battle" is a phony one. Both Republicans and Democrats subscribe to the idea that the government has a "responsibility" to ensure that all children and adults have health care. The Republicans are for only a "little bit" of coercion as a moral imperative; the Democrats are more consistent, wanting to enact a coercive program that would entrap everyone, with no spending limits at all. Most Democrats and Republicans never learn that, in politics, an innocuous amount of force is always an overture to wholesale force. The shrewder ones do know.

The "private sector" mentioned in the article is already heavily regulated and subsidized. One would have thought that it was the "responsibility" of children's parents – the unnamed portion of that "private sector" – to take care of their children, and not a federal or state Nurse Ratched. But rarely do parents enter the picture of national health proposals (except as tax cows).

As evidence of the Republicans' ignorance of what a "little bit" of coercion logically entails, consider the nature of Bush's "ideological" opposition to the congressional bill, as reported by the *Los Angeles Times*:

"He continued to describe the measure that he vetoed as 'deeply flawed,' contending that the plan was 'an incremental step toward their [the Democrats'] goal of government-run health care for every American,' which he believes is 'the wrong direction for our country.'"

Which direction is that? Bush did not say. He dared not say.

What he meant was *socialized medicine*, a term rarely employed by most politicians today. I can recall Republican presidential candidate Rudy Giuliani using it once, perhaps twice. Bush, however, did not want to accuse the Democrats of advocating it. After all, if he is willing to compromise with the bill's proponents and supporters, calling them closet socialists wouldn't make negotiations easy, and he doesn't want to appear to be against health care for children, not the advocate of "No Child Left Behind."

And the Democrats do not want to alert Americans that this is exactly what they have in mind. So the term has been swept under the thick rug of populist rhetoric. How childish of these adults to believe that if one doesn't name a thing, it can't exist, that it isn't what one means, that it can't be or won't ever be.

One of the bill's interesting provisions is that it would discourage states from "enrolling children in families that earn more than $60,000 a year." Do the bill's authors believe that a household income of $60,000 a year puts the earner in the same income bracket with Bill Gates or George Soros? Do they mean $60,000 before or after taxes, not including all the hidden and direct sales and excise taxes that the average household pays day in and day out? In 1910, $60,000 might have been a small fortune (and it would have been in genuine, non-inflatable gold and silver, no less); to consider $60,000 in fiat, paper money a fortune is too laughable an idea to even dwell on.

It is especially laughable when one knows that every Congressman and Senator pulls in far, far more than $60,000 a year, without performing a single day of productive, wealth-producing labor. Who came up with the arbitrary $60,000 figure? Ted Kennedy, living off his family's ill-gotten fortune and who has voted for and supported every piece of anti-American welfare legislation in his long and disreputable career? John Edwards, the glorified ambulance chaser who made his millions in medical malpractice suits? Multi-millionaire Hillary Clinton, whose transparent duplicity and power-lust are driving her political campaign?

Another interesting provision of the bill is that it would "boost tobacco taxes, raising the levy on cigarettes by 61 cents to $1 a pack."

Remember the big tobacco industry "master agreement" of yore? It was supposed to fill state coffers so states could combat alleged tobacco-related illnesses and browbeat children and adults about the dangers of smoking. The tobacco industry is still coughing up billions, but all that money shortly was consumed by other state priorities and is still going to programs and pork barrels of the legislators' eclectic choosings. Practically the only anti-tobacco ads one sees on television now are produced and paid for by Philip Morris.

On October 2, the Ayn Rand Institute published an Op-Ed by Don Watkins, "Anti-Smoking Paternalism: A Cancer on American Liberty." It is worth quoting its opening paragraph:

"Across the country, state and local governments are banning smoking on private property, including bars, restaurants, and office buildings. This is just the latest step in the government's war on smoking – a coercive campaign that includes massive taxes on cigarettes, advertising bans, and endless multi-billion lawsuits against tobacco companies. This war is infecting America with a political disease far worse than any health risk caused by smoking; it is destroying our freedom to make our own judgments and choices."

Mr. Watkins can be forgiven for overlooking recent smoking bans in cars with kids as passengers and even outside one's own home. Also worth mentioning are the fines and/or jail time some localities impose on adults for buying cigarettes for teens working "undercover" for cops.

The subject of raising the tobacco tax merits more examination. About 70% of the price of any pack of cigarettes represents a combined levy of federal, state and local taxes, just as about 60% of the price of a gallon of gas represents mostly federal tax. But one of the alleged purposes of the "sin tax" on especially cigarettes is to discourage smokers from smoking, and coerce them into living "healthier" lives.

This is presumably to enable them to better and more efficiently fund the welfare state; which means: living for the state. The contradictory conflict in ends should be obvious here – call it statist schizophrenia – that a dramatic rise in the cigarette tax is supposed to both fund either the Democrats' $60 billion expansion of the welfare state or Bush's $30 billion version, *and* also help stamp out smoking.

Hypothetically speaking, if the anti-smoking campaign is successful in stamping out smoking, with the consequence that the tax generates little or no tobacco revenue to the government, what do the health care bill's supporters think will fund this five-year program? Where will the money come from?

One errs when one thinks that legislators think beyond a certain effect. But behind such pernicious, liberty-destroying legislation is their knowledge that there are plenty of other "sins" being committed by the population that can be taxed. Foods loaded with trans-fats. Gas. The Internet. Telephone usage. The possibilities are endless.

The welfare of children has often served as a Trojan horse for legislation that eventually is extended to cover adults, from child labor laws to minimum wage laws to medical care for the elderly. Children are viewed by most politicians and advocates of paternalistic and collectivist legislation as helpless in an adult world. But, as Don Watkins points out in his Op-Ed, it is only a matter of time before the government views adults as unprotected, helpless and ignorant, as well, needing the velvet-lined mailed fist of government to oversee their welfare.

> "To the extent the anti-smoking movement succeeds in wielding the power of government coercion to impose on Americans its blanket opposition to smoking, it is entrenching *paternalism:* the view that individuals are incompetent to run their own lives, and thus require a nanny-state to control every aspect of those lives."

Sideshows such as the proposed expansion of the State Children's Health Insurance Program have a tendency to become three-ring circuses, featuring the looted in one ring, the loot's recipients in another, and in the middle a master of ceremonies wielding a whip, barking platitudes about sacrifice and the public good.

October 2007

Obama's Assault on the Mind

White House press secretaries have earned the reputation over the last half dozen administrations of being practiced in the arts of obfuscation, deception and lying with straight faces as opaque as plastomar. The White House press corps, for their part, have become inured to the hyperbolic and elliptical rhetoric. Depending on whether the corps are friendly or hostile to the administration, individual members can read the subtexts of a press secretary's statements and, governed by their biases and subjectivist preferences, tailor their interpretations one way or the other and project them as kinda-sorta news or analyses of what may or may not be official policies or positions. Their talent is to describe a pea-soup fog. This is what passes for modern journalism.

The press corps of President Barack Obama's White House are not a true press corps. The majority of its members have betrayed their vocation and attend these rigged press conferences as a formality. The events seem to be more dumb-show and noise for groundlings than opportunities for news-gathering. One gets the sense that the White House would rather just dispense with the formality. The corps may as well be animated mannequins; they rise on cue to ask pre-screened questions of the press secretary or president; the latter will have prepared answers to those questions, the former is a skilled fog-making machine. Teleprompter or no teleprompter, nothing could be phonier than give-and-take spontaneity that may as well be rehearsed.

Former President George W. Bush at least had a modicum of honesty and, during his infrequent press conferences, faced a largely hostile press corps and did not do well. His advisors kept him off-stage as much as possible and let his press secretary run interference. But now the news media have largely become a collective shill for Obama's policies, allies who give him a free pass for his contradictions and flip-flop policies, and who can be trusted to pass on to the public the latest official ukase. If any one of them decides not to play ball, presumably he will be put on a press conference "do not recognize" list.

Robert Gibbs, 38, a career political creature, has been Obama's press secretary since January, and has worked for Obama before, during and after the latter's Senate days. It should come as no surprise that he was also press spokesman for Senator John Kerry and other Democratic politicians. While he is no Joseph Goebbels, the maniacal propaganda chief of Nazi Germany whose obfuscations, deceptions, and lies were dutifully repeated as news by an unfree press, Gibbs performs much the same role for a press that chooses to be unfree. As Goebbels did, as the "public image" managers of tyrants in the past have done, he helped to create the myth of infallibility and the populist persona of Barack Obama, and now is responsible for preserving them. In that unconscionable fraud he is aided by a largely obliging news media.

But cracks are appearing in the façade of Obama's "open presidency." They are becoming more and more evident in Gibbs. On May 27, in response to a blog statement by Newt Gingrich that Judge Sonia Sotomayor, Obama's nominee for the Supreme Court, ought to withdraw from consideration or be withdrawn because of racist and feminist remarks she made, Gibbs said something that was in the spirit of Goebbels. Responding to the Republicans' opposition to Sotomayor, one based on her past affiliations, her less than stellar record of understanding the Constitution or even being cognizant of it, her apparent hostility to white males, and the media-generated myth that she is the daughter of immigrants (who, being Puerto Ricans, were actually U.S. citizens) who rose by her own efforts against tremendous odds (but, like Obama, probably the beneficiary of affirmative action or racial, gender, or "diversity" quota policies). Gibbs said, in the innocuous, undramatic tone of a garage mechanic recommending a certain grade of engine oil:

> "I think it is probably important for anybody involved in this debate to be exceedingly careful with the way in which they've decided to describe different aspects of this impending confirmation."

Briefly, there is no "aspect" of Sotomayor's character or record which should be open to description, identification or debate. If anyone breaks that rule, Gibbs implied, the offending party will be smeared as a racist, bigot, and misogynist. Gibbs and chief-of-staff Rahm Emanuel are in charge of the White House machinery that can manufacture a backlash of outrage. Ask Sotomayor legitimate questions at your own risk. Her confirmation hearing will be a "debate" in name only. Besides, her confirmation is "impending," in the cards, a sure thing, so why bother dredging up inconvenient truths about her?

When you watch Gibbs fielding questions from the press corps, you do not have the sense that you are observing evil incarnate. You do not see a Goebbels-like maniac. What you see is a person who very likely never once placed a value on truth or honesty. You see a non-entity whose existence is assured by his willingness to obfuscate, deceive, lie and juggle banalities commensurate with his character and task. You see a human face that reflects little else but calculation of how best to say nothing that could be interpreted as an absolute, a nondescript face with blank, evasive eyes and a self-effacing manner that expects and gets the cooperation of his auditors in putting one over on themselves and on the whole country.

Whether Gibbs' warning to the Republicans not to press too hard on Sotomayor's qualifications to sit on the Supreme Court was a conscious flouting of the First Amendment -- he should know that even Senators have First Amendment rights that should not be threatened or abridged by a mere press secretary or anyone else, let alone by a president -- or was an impromptu rebuke that was insensible to that Amendment, is irrelevant. What matters is that, for a moment, in a handful of incautious but revealing words, the mask of respect for anyone's right to freedom of speech was dropped. His warning was aimed not just at Senators, Internet bloggers and Newt Gingrich, but at the press and the news media. It was an all-encompassing growl of disapproval of any questioning of the alleged wisdom of his employer and of resentment for any questioning of his own assertions.

In the real world, the one beyond the White House and Congress, one would not give anyone like Gibbs or his assertions a second thought. His ilk are many, mean, and small. But threats emanating from the representative of a man who is consciously wreaking destruction on this country, who is contemptuous of the Constitution, individual rights, private property, and freedom of speech, should not be taken as a matter of routine. This is not the first time Obama's gofers have warned individuals away from speaking out on certain issues and facts. Gibbs' statements are uttered with the tacit approval of the president. Neither the president, nor Gibbs, nor anyone else on the White House staff, wishes anyone to think and speak with any gravity about Sotomayor or to trouble her with inopportune questions, which, under oath, she must answer with possibly damaging truths, during Senate confirmation hearings or in any other setting. They are all prepared to take retaliatory measures if anyone does.

What remains to be seen is whether or not any member of the Senate committee will be brave enough to take his First Amendment rights seriously enough to pose a single inopportune question, one that may suggest why Obama is so ideologically comfortable with her.

Gibbs' admonitory "advice" to critics of Sotomayor is an order *not to think*. A prohibition of thought necessarily extends to a prohibition from action, in this instance, to voluntarily refrain from asking questions lest the White House become "exceedingly" nasty. After all, why bother thinking about a matter when one is proscribed from acting on it? It is a blatant and unforgivable attack on the mind. Further, Sotomayor's silence on Gibbs' mealy-mouth diktat speaks volumes about her own position on the issue of the First Amendment; she does not seem to be aware that Gibbs violated it, or perhaps she is hoping that no one has noticed.

But, then, that has been the constant leitmotif of Obama's conduct in office.

June 2009

Occupy the Money

"I think we've been too slow to realize [why] people our own age, with histories just like ours, going through all that state stuff, to be [*sic*] dishonest, unprincipled, back-stabbing sleaze balls....Well, I was prejudiced in their favor. I thought that because they looked like us, and talked like us, they were going to think like us." (*The Big Chill*, 1983)

So whined an ex-radical from the protest movements of the 1960's and 1970's, at a reunion of ex-radicals on the occasion of the funeral of a former comrade, "Alex," who committed suicide and who was apparently the only one who "fought on." Most of the characters in Lawrence Kasdan's film of post-"revolutionary soul-searching over how they were "co-opted" by the "establishment" and now all lead comfortable middle class lives. That is, they had to actually support themselves.

Well, sir, they haven't stopped talking and thinking like "us." Taking a leaf from Saul Alinsky, they fought on. "There was only the fight." Now they're in power. They're the "establishment." You spoke too soon. You were dropped from the club of sleaze balls who ascended to the top and left you and your angst-ridden house-mates behind.

When the pond scum and bilge surfaced in American politics, you were not to be found in it.

Who would have thought, three or four decades ago, that Communist activists and terrorists such as Bill Ayers, Bernadine Dohrn, Van Jones, Anita Dunn, David Axelrod, Valerie Jarrett, Tom Haydn, Jane Fonda, and a gallery of other protégés, associates, appointees, and fellow travelers would become the social and political elite to formulate, determine and oversee domestic and foreign policies of the United States? Early on, in their violent and demonstrating heyday, they were virtually penniless, or the progeny of well-to-do parents. Now they bask in relative luxury, either as respected and tenured "academics," or thanks to their munificently compensated government appointments, or as heads of liberal non-profit organizations, or even as executives of multi-million dollar corporations.

They are not whining. How did they do it? Was it a conspiracy, or did they just fill a moral and political vacuum?

In "The Storm Troopers of OWS" last November, I noted that:

Occupy Wall Street was no spontaneous phenomenon, but a planned and organized instance of "community organizing," on a scale that would make Saul Alinsky proud. It is orchestrated anarchy intended to cripple the "system," careening towards whatever target its mobs reach a consensus to freeze, personalize, isolate, and polarize, angling for "confrontation" with the police that would put them in the role of "victims of violence" – when they are the initiators of force. One OWS chant is, "The whole world is watching."

Who are in the ranks of the OWS?

OWS is an amalgam of communists, welfare state liberals, old school radicals, gray panther leftists, new age hippies, holders of worthless degrees, the professionally unemployed, the perpetually alienated, the clinically certifiably disgruntled, career vagrants, vehicles of middle class guilt, black power advocates, Muslims, anti-Semites, Hispanics of indeterminate national origin, unions, AmeriCorps manqués, Peace Corps veterans, environmentalists – all the bilious movements that mushroomed on the mulch of American educational philosophy, and which were prepared and sanctioned by grade and high schools and universities and patronized, idolized, and encouraged by the news media.

And what did the mobs of the OWS want?

The variety of protest signs, usually scrawled on cardboard, often revealing a profound illiteracy in spelling and grammar, testify to the unity of "angst and anger" and the triumph of a university education. OWS brandishes a variety of banners, including the American, but the Palestinian and Puerto Rican flags were also in evidence. On the whole, what OWS is rebelling against is reality, but it is a reality their elective ilk have created.

OWS has in its ranks countless individuals ready to emulate the German Free Corps of post-World War I Germany. The paramilitary Free Corps helped to elevate Adolf Hitler to power. Many of them made the easy transition from the Free Corps to the SA and SS once the Nazis began to gather electoral steam. Many others found employment in other departments and programs of the Nazi Party.

OWS does not boast uniforms or paramilitary discipline. Its legions have not been street-fighting Communists, but rather have been jockeying for confrontations with the police, so that "all the world" would witness the altercation. But the absence of uniforms and discipline is irrelevant. There is no fundamental difference between the OWS and the Free Corps.

How did Hitler finance his rise to power? There are parallels to explore.

OWS is preparing Phase II of its clamorous and disruptive calls for "change." Phase II will require money. Aside from the usual suspects of George Soros affiliated donors, there is the usual assortment of affiliated fools, such as Ben & Jerry's founders Ben Cohen and Jerry Greenfield. The Wall Street Journal of February 28th has this interesting story:

A group of business leaders—including Ben Cohen and Jerry Greenfield of Ben & Jerry's ice cream and former Nirvana manager Danny Goldberg—are planning to pour substantial funds into the Occupy Wall Street movement in hopes of sustaining the protests and fostering political change.

> Their goal is to provide some ballast to an amorphous movement that captured the world's attention with nonstop, overnight protests in dozens of cities but has had trouble regaining momentum since most of those encampments were broken up by police in the past few months.

OWS has gone "formal," creating a mother ship of finance and guidance. No more of that rowdy, unsanitary, chaotic come-by-chance organization for them. It has "incorporated."

> The latest Occupy supporters call themselves the Movement Resource Group and have raised about $300,000 so far to parcel out in grants to protesters, said Mr. Cohen. Their goal is to raise $1.8 million.

Cohen and Greenfield were not protesting "radicals" of yore, though early photographs of them would lead one to believe they had been right in there battling police and inhaling tear gas and risking thwacks on the head by nightsticks and batons.

Nevertheless, they were "radicals," and still are.

> A little more than two-thirds [of the $1.8 million] was donated by the Ben & Jerry's Foundation and members of the group's steering committee, which includes Dal Lamagna, founder of the company

Tweezerman, entertainment-industry executive Richard Foos and Judy Wicks, founder of the White Dog Café in Philadelphia, along with Messrs. Cohen, Greenfield and Goldberg.

The remainder—about $60,000—came from individual donors, including Norman Lear, a television producer and philanthropist, and Terri Gardner, former president and chief executive of Soft Sheen hair products.

Some entrepreneurs and successful businessmen will gladly provide the rope with which they will eventually be hanged. Norman Lear? Got to keep those "Meat Heads" all in the family.

"Many of us have been working for progressive social change," Mr. Cohen, a prominent supporter of liberal causes, said Monday. "There's been a critical ingredient missing."

Such as better coordination, a focused agenda, and better-trained troops. Perhaps an escrow account for attorney's fees and bail bonds.

The group will give grants of as much as $25,000 to protesters across the country after undergoing an application process that begins in March. The group, along with five Occupy activists, will review applications.

Of the money raised so far, $150,000 will pay for rent and equipment for an office in New York for the national Occupy movement. An additional $100,000 has been set aside for individual project proposals, and a small portion of the money has been set aside to provide stipends for people Mr. Cohen describes as "core activists."

Still, the dog insists on, if not biting the hands that feed it, then growling at it in dissatisfaction. There were complaints about the donations.

Mr. Cohen and other members of the group met with protesters in a Manhattan church Sunday night to pitch the idea to dedicated activists. Not all were impressed, on the theory it would only add bureaucracy.

"Essentially this is a group of very wealthy people who have picked a handler to deal with Occupy Wall Street," said Ravi Ahmed, 34 years old, a protester who works as an academic administrator. "They've re-created what's wrong with nonprofits and philanthropy structures."

What's wrong with the whole system is that without all the iPods, and cell phones, tents, and shoes, and processed food and Starbucks, and especially ice cream, not to mention cardboard on which to scrawl semi-literate protests with Magic Markers and dime-store stencils – all that and more produced by wealthy people and used by OWSers to facilitate their protest against "wealthy people" – where would Mr. Ahmed and his colleagues be? Would they even exist? But, these are subjects beyond the ken of OWSers.

And what is actually wrong with most nonprofits and philanthropies is that they are largely altruistic and leftist vehicles to distribute wealth their administrators never created. Watch the credits for any PBS television program about the plight of penguins or polar bears or rain forests, or the struggles of Mexican-Americans and Muslims to retain their "culture," or the aspirations of inner-city graffiti artists and gang members; it is a roll call of guileless and guilt-ridden "humanitarians."

Ben & Jerry's isn't in the same league as Krupp, German industrialists, bankers and manufacturers. But the German magnates and moneyed elite were also bitten by their beneficiaries. It's a difference in scale but the ends are the same.

Many years ago, Antony C. Sutton, a British-born "rogue historian," produced a three-volume blockbusting study under the auspices of the Hoover Institution at Stanford University of why the Soviet Union was able to stumble through seventy years of existence in spite of its mass murders, its vast gulag of prisons for dissenters, its chronic crop failures, its crippled industrial base, and a lethargic population of "workers," *Western Technology and Soviet Economic Development.* In this remarkable study Sutton demonstrated how the Soviets were chiefly thieves and copycats in every major technological and industrial field, and that much of the thieving and copycatting was abetted by Western industrialists, bankers, and politicians.

Sutton made the same revealing and thoroughly documented study of the origins of the Nazi Party and its financial underpinnings, *Wall Street and the Rise of Hitler,* detailing as well Hitler's ability to command the whole German economy once the Party was in power.

We do know that prominent European and American industrialists were sponsoring all manner of totalitarian political groups at that time, including Communists and various Nazi groups. The [post-WW2] U.S. Kilgore Committee records that:

By 1919 Krupp was already giving financial aid to one of the reactionary political groups which sowed the seed of the present Nazi ideology. Hugo Stinnes was an early contributor to the Nazi Party (National Socialistische Deutsche Arbeiter Partei). *By 1924 other prominent industrialists and financiers, among them Fritz Thyssen, Albert Voegler, Adolph* [sic] *Kirdorf, and Kurt von Schroder, were secretly giving substantial sums to the Nazis. In 1931 members of the coal-owners' association which Kirdorf headed pledged themselves to pay 50 pfennigs for each ton of coal sold, the money to go to the organization which Hitler was building.*

Reading about the humble donations of Ben Cohen and Jerry Greenfield, and their concerns about OWS's future as a mover and shaker for "social change" is a let-down, when we can see how big-scale financing of a mover and shaker was done in Germany.

In 1925 the Hugo Stinnes family contributed funds to convert the Nazi weekly *Volkischer Beobachter* to a daily publication. [Ernst] Putzi Hanfstaengl, Franklin D. Roosevelt's friend and protegé, provided the remaining funds. Table 7-1 summarizes presently known financial contributions and the business associations of contributors from the United States. Putzi is not listed in Table 7-1 as he was neither industrialist nor financier.

In the early 1930s financial assistance to Hitler began to flow more readily. There took place in Germany a series of meetings, irrefutably documented in several sources, between German industrialists, Hitler himself, and more often Hitler's representatives Hjalmar Sehaeht and Rudolf Hess.

The critical point is that the German industrialists financing Hitler were predominantly directors of cartels with American associations, ownership, participation, or some form of subsidiary connection. The Hitler backers were not, by and large, firms of purely German origin, or representative of German family business. Except for Thyssen and Kirdoff, in most cases they were the German multi-national firms — *i.e., I.G.* Farben, A.E.G.,

DAPAG, *etc.* These multi-nationals had been built up by American loans in the 1920s, and in the early 1930s had American directors and heavy American financial participation.

America has not seen the last of Occupy Wall Street. Like a spoiled, unruly brat who fouls his own nest on principle, the organization and its hierarchy are being preened for a more active role in American politics. This takes money, guidance, organization and very sophisticated press agentry. For an almost amusing story of the aimlessness and infighting among OWSers, read the New York Post's story from last October, "They Want a $lice of the Occupie," an aimlessness and inner-ranks conflict that "new money" hopes to correct.

As for George Soros's connection with OWS, Reuters published an insipid exposé that merely scratches the surface:

> Soros and the protesters deny any connection. But Reuters did find indirect financial links between Soros and Adbusters, an anti-capitalist group in Canada which started the protests with an inventive marketing campaign aimed at sparking an Arab Spring type uprising against Wall Street. Moreover, Soros and the protesters share some ideological ground.

> The Hungarian-American was an early supporter of the 2008 election campaign of Barack Obama, who will seek a second term as president in the November, 2012, election. He has long backed liberal causes - the Open Society Institute, the foreign policy think tank Council on Foreign Relations and Human Rights Watch.

> According to disclosure documents from 2007-2009, Soros' Open Society gave grants of $3.5 million to the Tides Center, a San Francisco-based group that acts almost like a clearing house for other donors, directing their contributions to liberal non-profit groups. Among others the Tides Center has partnered with are the Ford Foundation and the Gates Foundation.

> Disclosure documents also show Tides, which declined comment, gave Adbusters grants of $185,000 from 2001-2010, including nearly $26,000 between 2007-2009.

> Aides to Soros say any connection is tenuous and that Soros has never heard of Adbusters. Soros himself declined comment.

As tenuous a connection as a pit bull latched onto one's leg. News Busters, however, not a member of the MSM, goes into far more detail:

> Reuters even posed the question "Who's behind the Wall St. protests?" on Oct. 13, but downplayed Soros's actual financial involvement. Even though "Soros and the protesters share some ideological ground," the story added. But Reuters undersold the connection significantly.
>
> The protesters stand by their claim that theirs is purely a grassroots movement. But it is hard to ignore the concerted effort by liberal groups, unions, and other Soros-funded entities that prop-up and fuel the Occupy movement. An echo-chamber of left-wing blogs and news sites that receive Soros cash continues to push the anti-capitalist protest story. Articles repeatedly praise labor and climate activists for their support while denigrating police for their efforts to keep the peace.
>
> Organizations that joined the protesters were granted more than $3.6 million from Soros's Open Society Foundations. On Oct. 5 there was a "march in solidarity with #occupywallstreet" that listed seven such groups out of the 16 overall supporting the protest. Those seven organizations received $3,614,690 from Soros' Open Society Foundations since the year 2000, with more than $2 million going to Common Cause Education Fund, part of Common Cause, and another $1.1 million to MoveOn.org.

This writer does not subscribe to conspiracy theories. He puts more credence and the onus of responsibility on a moral and philosophical vacuum that collectivist plotters and actors are only too happy to fill. If there were a proper, principled defense of individual rights and the inviolate sanctity of an unadulterated Constitution, plotters and conspirators could act all they wished and would be foiled by such a defense. But what we are seeing unfolding before our eyes, with not much of an alarm being raised, as far as OWS is concerned, is simply a rerun of what happened in Germany, with a whole new cast of directors and actors.

Imagine Leni Riefenstahl's *Triumph of the Will* remade in the spirit of *Hair*.

Nobody said that fascism had to speak German and wear shirts and ties when it resurfaced. And nobody ever claimed that communism, or its national-socialist doppelganger, had to speak Russian and wear fur hats, either to march in the streets.

All it has taken, ever since the rise of totalitarian ideologies in the 20th century, is a little cash under the table to help make things happen.

March 2012

Thomas Ricks Wants Your Kids

Just when you thought the government was finished scheduling your life and mapping out how you can become an exemplar of gung-ho "giving back" citizenship, another Pulitzer Prize winner concocts still another scheme to best exploit your life, time, and energies. One couldn't imagine a better way to complement the passage of Obamacare and the Supreme Court's upholding it on the notion that penalties are taxes and taxes are penalties than by proposing a new, improved, and eminently fair and cost-saving draft.

After all, if we are now all officially wards of the state, why not? If doctors and other medical professionals can be *de facto* drafted to serve as serfs, why not your children?

Brought to my attention by Daniel Greenfield in his July 14th Sultan Knish column was Thomas R. Ricks's New York Times opinion piece of July 9th, "Let's Draft Our Kids." Greenfield handily dismisses most of Ricks's proposals as the ravings of an ignoramus and lunatic, but I saw something else in Ricks's article that beggared comment. What Ricks is proposing is a scheme for indentured servitude that makes the old Roosevelt era Civilian Conservation Corps look like a Boy Scout jamboree.
Richard M. Salsman, in his Forbes article, "A Finalized Path to Full, Socialized Medicine in America – Thanks to Conservatives," on the Supreme Court's ruling, noted on June 28th that:

> With today's ruling the U.S. government can do virtually anything it wishes to its citizens – liberty and rights be damned, without limit. Officially in America we now have a totally arbitrary and limitless government. That is, we have a "total government." In short, we've got *totalitarian* government. As to how much further liberty we may lose in our lifetimes, it'll depend only on how arbitrary and vicious reigning rulers choose to be, or not. There's no real Rule of Law any more, only the Rule of Men – and these are mostly ignorant, reckless men.

Greenfield regards Ricks as one of those ignorant, reckless men, brimming with collectivist schemes to bring about the full employment of a generation fresh from indoctrination and epistemological lobotomization in the public schools. Greenfield, for example, quotes Ricks:

A revived draft, including both males and females, should include three options for new conscripts coming out of high school. Some could choose 18 months of military service with low pay but excellent post-service benefits, including free college tuition. These conscripts would not be deployed but could perform tasks currently outsourced at great cost to the Pentagon: paperwork, painting barracks, mowing lawns, driving generals around, and generally doing lower-skills tasks so professional soldiers don't have to. If they want to stay, they could move into the professional force and receive weapons training, higher pay and better benefits.

Greenfield: That "great cost" would clearly be more than balanced by taking hundreds of thousands of teens out of the work force and then paying for their college tuition and health care for life, so that they can do paperwork and paint barracks... even though we can already find volunteers to do this already. And in a shocking turn of events, those volunteers would actually choose military service as part of their career plan.
Those who don't want to serve in the army could perform civilian national service for a slightly longer period and equally low pay — teaching in low-income areas, cleaning parks, rebuilding crumbling infrastructure, or aiding the elderly. After two years, they would receive similar benefits like tuition aid.

Greenfield: So now we're drafting people into a national workforce to clean parks in low income areas? Or we could just use paroled prisoners, long-term welfare cases and bored liberal kids for that.

And what about "conscientious objectors" who don't wish to become indistinguishable elements in the Fascist *gestalt*? What will happen to individuals who value their lives, liberty, property and pursuits of their selfish happiness? Why, they'll be "free" to choose their fates.

And libertarians who object to a draft could opt out. Those who declined to help Uncle Sam would in return pledge to ask nothing from him — no Medicare, no subsidized college loans and no mortgage guarantees. Those who want minimal government can have it.

Greenfield:... sounds reasonable. So long as they wouldn't be expected to pay into the system and get tax discounts so they don't have to pay for anybody else's Medicare, college loans and mortgages for low income areas.

That is, those who don't "volunteer" to serve or who resist conscription will be left to sleep under bridges in discarded cardboard containers and root through garbage bins for scraps of food. In such a society of servitude, individualists will become pariahs and outcasts in their own country – the country founded to protect individual rights. Universal conscription such as Ricks proposes is a prescription for slavery and poverty.

That aspect of Ricks's idea is fundamentally unworkable, as any Alinskyite, fully committed Marxist, or wannabe Nazi will tell you. Those who do not "volunteer" will be forced to choose their mode of servitude. Totalitarians and totalitarianism do not offer anyone optional alternatives. It is but a short leap from "community organizing" to "national organizing." Ask the White House.

It is tempting to suspect that Ricks is probably enamored of that awful Denise Richards vehicle, "Starship Troopers," in which boys and girls donned combat gear to fight telekinetic insects from across the galaxy. In exchange for that "service," and if they survived, they'd get free college education and other societal perks, as well. Or perhaps Ricks dreamed up his scheme from having watched Occupy Wall Streeters demonstrate and riot and engage in criminal actions.

"Very nice kids," he might have thought. "But they've got to be channeled into more constructive participation in our democracy."

Ricks is a fellow at the Center for a New American Security, a contributing editor to Foreign Policy magazine, and also the author of several books on the military and military policies. The woozy mission statement of the CNAS betrays it as a left-wing "think tank" dedicated to developing "strong, pragmatic and principled national security and defense policies." It's interesting that the mission statement contains the glaring contradiction of pragmatism and principles. But I could detect nothing substantive in the rest of what the CNAS purports to accomplish.

What inspired Ricks to wax ignorantly on the "benefits" of a new system of compulsory servitude were the remarks of former top commander of coalition forces in Afghanistan, General Stanley McChrystal in an interview on July 3rd, in Foreign Policy.

"I think we ought to have a draft. I think if a nation goes to war, it shouldn't be solely be represented by a professional force, because it gets to be unrepresentative of the population," McChrystal said at a late-night event June 29 at the 2012 Aspen Ideas Festival. "I think if a nation goes to war, every town, every city needs to be at risk. You make that decision and everybody has skin in the game."

So, we should complement a volunteer force with mobs of conscripts in order to be "representative of the population"? Representative of what? Or of whom? Income classes? Levels of literacy? Gender preferences? Since when was our military dubbed to be an instrument of social policy? Oh, that's right. The military has served as a "proving ground" for social policies for decades now. The Democrats especially have been busy emasculating it ever since Bill Clinton's turn in the White House.

He argued that the burdens of the wars in Iraq and Afghanistan haven't been properly shared across the U.S. population, and emphasized that the U.S. military could train draftees so that there wouldn't be a loss of effectiveness in the war effort.

So, the burden of sending "our kids" to serve in a military assigned to implement a foreign "social" policy of converting barbaric, backwater Muslim countries into "democracies," no matter the cost in their lives and dollars, should be more equitably shared by everyone. It was never in America's self-interest to invade Bosnia, Kuwait, Iraq, or Afghanistan except to retaliate against Islamic organizations and states that sponsored terrorism that had declared war on this country. But the Left has never approved of any war we have fought unless it was preeminently *selfless* and *sacrificing*.

McChrystal and Ricks are simply advocating a renewal of the policy originated by Woodrow Wilson and the Progressive wings of the Democrats and Republicans. About our entry into World War I, Sheldon Richman notes:

The messianic President Wilson could not pass up what he saw as a once-in-a-lifetime opportunity to help remake the world. As historian Arthur Ekirch writes in *The Decline of American Liberalism,* "The notion of a crusade came naturally to Wilson, the son of a Presbyterian minister, imbued with a stern Calvinist sense of determinism and devotion to duty." He was goaded by a host of Progressive intellectuals, such as John Dewey and Herbert Croley,

73

editor of *The New Republic*, who wrote that "the American nation needs the tonic of a serious moral adventure."

....Within months, the United States had conscription, an official propaganda office, suppression of dissent, and central planning of the economy (a precedent for Franklin Roosevelt's New Deal).

While Richman's thesis, which lays blame on the Treaty of Versailles of 1919 for the rise of Nazi Germany, opposes Ludwig von Mises's thesis that Germany was properly blamed and punished for the war (and I happen to support the von Mises thesis, which can be found in *Omnipotent Government*, reviewed here), Richman's assertion that the active involvement of the United States in European political affairs laid the groundwork for the next war and for our own brand of statism, is valid.

It is John Dewey's educational philosophy that governs American public schools today, while Herbert Croly, a Progressive, wrote the blueprint for American fascism, *The Promise of American Life*, in 1909. In it, he claimed that "the traditional American confidence in individual freedom has resulted in a morally and socially undesirable distribution of wealth," and that it was time for the federal government to become more aggressive in economic planning and to assign Americans a better reason for living and working than for their own selfish purposes. Croly explicitly recommended that the United States move from freedom to "corporate (crony) capitalism" and from a Constitutionally limited government to the welfare state. These are the principal characteristics of Fascism.

Thomas Ricks is the trollish heir to the policies advocated by Wilson, Dewey, and Croly in the last century. Nothing he proposes is new or original, as collectivist programs go, except that it proposes to harness the military as the vehicle of servitude. However, the sanctioning of totalitarianism by the Supreme Court and the formal scrapping of the Constitution by the Court have allowed him to come out of the Progressive closet to float his trial balloon of universal conscription.

That his brazen proposals would necessitate a greater national debt is irrelevant. Greenfield in his Sultan Knish column also points out Ricks's utterly reckless ignorance of the dollar costs of his scheme. All collectivist schemes are costly. Costs have never troubled collectivists. But it would be easy to imagine Ricks's appointment to a new Federal Bureau of Human Resources, in which he would lord it over the lives of young people by sending them hither and yon in national service. He would be a natural fit for this new "czardom."

He would also be a perfect companion for another totalitarian, Kathleen Sibelius, Secretary of the Department of Health and Human Resources. In 2011, Forbes named her "the most powerful woman in the world." And Thomas Ricks would become "the most powerful man in the world."

They could squabble amicably over where to send *you* and *your* children. And if you protested or resisted the new conscription, they could flip a coin to decide what to do with *you.*

July 2012

ISLAM

A Nexus of Nihilism

> "Political nihilism advocates the prior destruction of all existing political, social, and religious orders as a prerequisite for any future improvement," states one Internet site. "Existential nihilism, the most well-known view, affirms that life has no intrinsic meaning or value."

It should confound no one that the "atheistic" or "agnostic" liberal/left has found common ground with Islam, ostensively a religious creed, thus allying itself with political/religious ideology. How can this be, when they are so obviously antithetical? For brevity's sake, I use the term *socialism* throughout this commentary to stand for any of its variants: the liberal/left, communism, fascism, corporatism, or *any* political system that regards the individual as a mere cog of society, duty-bound to serve and sacrifice to it, and indebted to society and/or the state for his existence and well-being.

It is the thesis of this commentary that both socialism and Islam are forms of *political nihilism,* and that both contend that the life of the individual has no intrinsic meaning or value outside of their systems. One ascribes meaning to the individual as a unit of society and its servant, and no more than that. The other ascribes meaning to the individual as a debtor to and servant of a supreme being, and no more than that.

As demonstrated by the actions of President Barack Obama and a Democratic Congress over the last one and a half years, socialism (with fascist trappings) adheres to its purpose of destroying all existing political, social and economic orders as a prerequisite for any further improvement. This is and continues to be the goal of Obama's "hope and change."

As demonstrated by the alleged "extremists" of Islam, and by their "non-violent" brethren, Islam likewise seeks to destroy all existing political, social, economic, and religious orders as a prerequisite for any future improvement, which is a global caliphate in which all men submit to Islam, one way or another, or die..

These two ideologies have, for the moment, set aside their differences to work together until the common enemy, the West, is disabled, conquered, emasculated, and beaten. In the United States, it means to vitiate the Constitution, abandon the republican form of government, and institute some form of "pure" democracy. Under the secular brand, this would mean the manipulated (and bogus) rule of the "poor" and "needy" of all stripes and categories. Under Islam, it would mean ruling a subservient and obedient class of Muslims and a sub-class of conquered non-believers.

On the surface, Islam and socialism are discordant and irreconcilable opposites. In truth, they are rivals for political power, and only one can "win" in that contest. If Islam triumphs, "atheistic" and other non-believing socialists would be expected to convert and "submit" to the religious component of Islam, which is fundamentally a political/religious ideology, and to acknowledge Allah as the one and only "true" God and Mohammed as his prophet. Barring conversion, the socialist must accept the status of a dhimmi and pay jizya, or a special tax on non-believers. He will exist at the pleasure of Islam. The only other alternative offered by Islam is death.

Islam is no stranger to socialism. In fact, as Daniel Pipes and other observers have noted, Islam has made common cause with communism and socialism in the past. Islamic scholars and intellectuals have endorsed socialist trends in countries they wished to see Islam triumph. The phenomenon of America's liberal/left making cause with Islam is just another episode of that on-again and off-again alliance.

If socialism wins, Islam is no worse off. It can exist in a socialist political/economic environment and bide its time, unless totalitarian measures are taken by the state to eradicate Islam as a rival ideology. The Soviet Union for decades suppressed both Christianity and Islam and all manner of other religions. Under socialism, everyone, including Muslims, would need to acknowledge the state or some personification of it (e.g., "Big Brother") or some other prominent person and advocate of collectivism as the "true" God or "savior, and Karl Marx or Mao or Lenin as the "prophet." Opposition to or digression from such deference and worship in any form would be deemed heresy, or blasphemy, and be punished with repression, imprisonment, or death.

If the West is sundered and vanquished, the two species of totalitarianism will fight savagely over the carcass, just as Hitler and Stalin fought over the carcass of Eastern Europe. That, of course, would be the beginning of a new Dark Age. Let us not forget the hundreds of thousands of "illegal" Catholic Mexicans pouring into this country. Will they convert to Islam or put up a fight? The totality of Islamic totalitarianism means just that: *everyone and everything*. Let us not forget America's "native Americans," or the Indians, and Catholic South America, and Australia and New Zealand, and the whole of the African continent. Islam is committed to a global caliphate. That means everyone and everything coming under its rule. If the West collapses, it will be a bloody and horrendous Dark Age.

Why has the liberal/left formed a "gentlemen's agreement" alliance with Islam? Islam opposed communism in Afghanistan, but one suspects that was mere opposition to a rival totalitarian ideology, not for sovereignty reasons. What would Islam profess to see it has in common with a strain of secular statism? What would advocates of secular statism profess to see it has in common with a political/religious ideology?

What are the commonalities of secular statism (or socialism) and Islam? What premises do they share? What are their shared ends? Are those ends similar or dissimilar or radically divergent?

The ends are demonstrably dissimilar and divergent. What unites them?

One thing stands out: The liberal/left, of its own accord and without evidence of an invitation, sides with Islam on several issues. There is Supreme Court appointee Elena Kagan and her penchant for Sharia law. There is Keith Ellison, Muslim representative from Minnesota. There is Barack Obama, who has a Muslim background and who has initiated an "outreach" to the Muslim world in a way he has not "reached out" to the Christian or secular world (except to pick its pockets).

The chief commonality between socialism and Islam is the deep-seated hatred -- and I would say is *the* fundamental motive of both socialism and Islam, its desiderative *essence* -- of the West, specifically of capitalism, of individual rights, and of freedom of speech. And particularly of America. What is it about those three hallmarks of Western culture that arouses the shared animosity? They are the requirements of an independent, unobstructed, free-to-act, selfish, value-driven, and life-affirming man. They are the descriptive attributes that cannot be permitted in a totalitarian society. They are diametrically opposite of what secular statism and Islam require to function. They are the unified, integrated nemesis of collectivism. They do not describe the "ideal" man in either ideology. Such a man must be eradicated, destroyed. And once destroyed, such a man in either system cannot be permitted to come into existence.

Under either system, the individual is but an obedient, manipulated, exploited, unquestioning manqué.

Islamic or Sharia law commands that Muslims who convert to Christianity or otherwise become apostates must be killed (Redda Law); women found guilty of adultery must be stoned to death; men can beat and rape their wives as disciplinary measures; homosexuals should be killed. Several Muslim texts declare that Jews are pigs and monkeys; killing them before the end of the world is a religious duty for Muslims. Muslim texts, approved by all the schools of Islamic jurisprudence (Shafeii, Hanbali, Maleki, and Hanafi) state that Muslims must declare ceaseless wars against non-Muslims to spread Islam and those they conquer must either convert to Islam, pay jizya, or be killed.

The two brands of *jihad* -- violent and stealth -- must continue until the whole world is contained in the Islamic Ummah. Then there will be peace. An Islamic, totalitarian peace.

This is nihilism. Islam knows the good, and wishes to destroy it for the sake of its destruction. To replace it with a form of mass, universal zombie-ism, a society of the living dead.

Not something the left/liberals much contemplate. They are focused on the short-term gain of destroying the existing orders. The zealots of Islam, however, do not much contemplate their rival ideology or its practitioners. They are not concerned with the doctrines of socialism. They practically endorse them in their literature. They, too, wish to destroy the existing orders, to subjugate the individual in mind and body as thoroughly as the secular statists wish to. Should they lose the contest for power, they will continue to exist. They know that should they win the contest, their rivals will not be around for long.

The secular statists wish to destroy the good, as well, and replace the "existing order" with a zombie-populated mechanistic one that functions automatically in defiance of social and economic laws. In defiance of reality. This, too, is a nihilistic goal. They wish everyone to wade in the sump of socialism and be happy with what deleterious effluvia "society" provides them.

But, which is the more perilous ideology? Does one oppose Islam or socialism first? Or both at the same time? Which is more heinous, which is to be feared the most?

Observe cause and effect. When reason and Aristotelian philosophy governed the West, Islam was a fringe religion practiced in the uncivilized hell holes and backwaters of the world. Its practices of extortion, slavery, and brutality were beyond the pale of rational existence. It had no power to conquer the West or make any inroads in or demands on Western culture. There were no stagings in Muslim madrassas of a mullah-approved version of Mozart's "Abduction from the Seraglio," no Offenbach-like can-cans performed by women in smothering burqas or any other proscribed garb. No Muslim St. Gaudens sculpting Diana the Hunter, nor an Abdullah Hill building a private railroad across the Arabian wastes. The philosophy of life and living enjoyed in the West was incongruent, impossible, and antithetical to life under Islam. Winston Churchill observed just how deadening the religion was (and still is).

> How dreadful are the curses which Mohammedanism lays on its votaries! Besides the fanatical frenzy, which is as dangerous in a man as hydrophobia in a dog, there is this fearful fatalistic apathy....Individual Moslems may show splendid qualities. Thousands become the brave and loyal soldiers of the Queen: all know how to die. But the influence of the religion paralyzes the social development of those who follow it. No stronger retrograde force exists in the world. Far from being moribund, Mohammedanism is a militant and proselytizing faith. It has already spread throughout Central Africa, raising fearless warriors at every step; and were it not that Christianity is sheltered in the strong arms of science - the science against which it had vainly struggled - the civilization of modern Europe might fall, as fell the civilization of ancient Rome.

When the West began to abandon reason, at first piecemeal, then wholesale as it did throughout the twentieth century, all kinds of political and social pug-uglies began knocking on the West's door. Islam began to acquire influence and an ascending momentum.

In short, socialism, or secular statism, adopted as a continuing political policy in the West, together with its destructive offspring, egalitarianism and multiculturalism, facilitated the invasion of and ascendancy of "radical" Islam, and in combination fostered the growth of competing ideologies of La Raza, black power, and other strains of collectivism.

Were it not for the multiculturalism, egalitarianism, and unlimited government power to impose such policies on America, to favor one group over another -- that is, the power to "level" the playing field to advance one alleged minority over another, in exchange for reciprocal support for the bestowers and dispensers of such favors at polling places -- Islam, La Raza, all the various beneficiaries of "group rights," would remain, if they existed at all, on the farthest fringes of a free, civilized society, impotent by virtue of their inherent irrationalism.

All this has been examined before by professional intellectuals and perceptive observers, sometimes profitably, other times not. But I sense that the paradoxical nexus of today's left/liberal alliance with Islam remains an insoluble paradox. However, I have a detective hero whose operating motto is, "Nothing that is observable in reality is exempt from rational scrutiny." His specialty is to solve what I call "moral paradoxes."

The left/liberal-Islam axis is a paradox that will remain one only to those who defer to the inscrutable in their lives, their economics, their philosophy. They are the ones who will end up slaves, or dead. They are the ultimate facilitators and enablers of the nihilists.

August 2010

Allah's Oops!

Salman Rushdie, author of *The Satanic Verses*, a chaotic and bewildering novel which earned him a permanent death fatwa by Ayatollah Ruhollah Khomeini in February 1989, will attend a literary conference in New Delhi, India in March, in defiance of Islamic naysayers. We can credit him with the defiance, but not his *oeuvre* with literary worth. I signed a petition in 1989 that opposed the fatwa and called on Western governments to uphold freedom of speech, a petition inspired by Khomeini's death sentence on Rushdie and on anyone who dared defend him or promote his book.

Out of curiosity, I tried reading *The Satanic Verses*, and one-quarter into it was unable and unwilling to finish it. I would liken it to a fantasy tale centered around the ribald adventures of believers in the merged worlds of the Rosicrucians and Yale's Skull and Bones secret society.

If it hadn't been for Khomeini's fatwa, as someone has noted elsewhere, Rushdie's novel would be gathering dust in second-hand bookstores, and Rushdie himself perhaps would be writing for The Daily Telegraph or the Guardian to earn a living.

So, what were those "Satanic Verses" that got the turbaned tyrants of Iran incensed? What is Sura 53 all about? It has to do with that obsession of inadequate and repressed Muslims everywhere: *women*! No wonder they're raped, and beaten, and disfigured, and reduced to fractions and invisibility! Allah was the original male chauvinist pig. But, never mind *The Satanic Verses*. Here is a less obtuse accounting of what *really* happened in seventh century Mecca.

*   *   *

Once upon a time Allah had three daughters. You heard right. Not one, but three daughters, and they were all as powerful as he. As goddesses, they were worshipped by Arabs before Mohammad put an end to that pagan polytheism. Their names were al-Lät, al-Uzza, and Manät. They were okay, said the Angel Gabriel to him in his sleep, or in his dreams, or in his ear. "They are the Sorority of Serenity Now! Sirens of the Belly-Dance. Top-drawer cunning vixens! Make offerings to them in their temples, and your wishes will be granted!"

That was the original Sura, as reported by early Islamic scholars. Mohammad of course was dictating the *Koran* and speaking as though in a trance (reciting what he was hearing, so to speak, or so he claimed), and his scribe hurriedly scratched it all down on parchment rescued from the looted Alexandrian Library, bleached of any blasphemy. Mohammad, the Billy Sunday of his day, had decided that the Meccans he was trying to convert to Islam liked variety in their deities. Why not keep some sexy seductresses, and add some spice to the creed?

At least, that's what he thought he thought, as he was listening to "the voice." Mohammad was of two minds: he was hearing voices, while his subconscious worked overtime to see how he could take advantage of what he was hearing.

Then he had a change of mind. Or Gabriel came to him again one night, chewed him out, and changed it for him. Gabriel peered over the scribe's shoulder and read the latest Sura. He exploded.

"You fool! You dunderhead! That wasn't *me* whispering in your ear last night! That was....*Shaytan*! I was in the Crab Nebula last night on other business, so *I* never told you that Allah had three daughters! I got a proper tongue-lashing from Allah this morning, thanks to your date-addled brain, you mewling kid of a camel, you spawn of a Jewess!"

Mohammad looked hurt and humiliated. He muttered under his breath, "Oops!"

Gabriel paced back and forth furiously, shaking his finger at Mohammad. "Now, listen up, chowder head! There is only one God, and his name is Allah! No goddesses! No daughters! No sons, either! Tell your scribe to cross out that Sura, and replace it with, 'Are men's children to be boys and Allah's to be girls? How unfair!' That's how it should read! Those are Allah's very words!"

Now, Mohammad wanted to establish a new religion, and be exalted for what remained of eternity as its infallible founder. Still, he found it a curiously awkward means to spread the Word, and the Word was Allah's. A rather roundabout way of revealing that Word to mortals he could not imagine, he would think in his most private moments. Allah speaks it to this snooty Angel, and the Angel whispers it to him, and he recites it to this bent-over, aging scribe. Not very time efficient.

Mohammad blinked in confusion. "But, oh, my Winged Whispering Wonder! What about al-Lät, and al-Uzza, and Manät? Do they not exist? Temples have been built for them, the yokels here have worshipped them for ages. Are we to have no variety in our worship? Allah is fine, as the Main Moon Man, but...people say it gets old, just worshipping one god. Why not a family of them?" He paused, and had a thought. "And if they are his daughters, who was their mother? We are missing a goddess, it would seem."

"What Shaytan told you was blasphemy!" shouted Gabriel. "There are no other gods! Only Allah! All other gods are figments of men's imaginations! Unreal! Without temporal or spiritual substance! Shape up, Mohammad, or Allah will choose another Prophet, and leave you to run with the dogs!"

Mohammad looked quizzical. He blurted, "Is Allah androgynous? Is he...without gender?"

Gabriel was stunned by this statement. Mohammad was illiterate. Where could he have picked up those words? But, he stepped up to Mohammad and slapped him silly, and so hard that the lice in the Prophet's beard jumped ship, and Mohammad's cheek was red for a day and a night. "How dare you question Allah's manhood, you filthy *jammal*! You pile of dog *chur*!"

But Gabriel otherwise did not answer the question. He remained in the tent long enough to make sure that Mohammad instructed the scribe to make the change. He could not instruct the scribe himself, because he was visible only to Mohammad, and could only be heard by the Prophet. Mohammad explained to the scribe that he got it wrong the first time, because of accumulated wax in his ear.

The scribe, of course, was accustomed to Mohammad talking to himself, or at least to the unseen and unheard Angel Gabriel. He sort of believed in the existence of the Angel, because, often as he scratched away on the parchment, he felt a cold presence weighing on his shoulders and breathing down his neck.

We are assuming that Gabriel was of the masculine suasion. The Bible tells us so. Or perhaps not.

Before he went poof and vanished, the Angel Gabriel pulled from inside his robes a long, curved object. "Here," he said. "With this you will conquer Arabia, if all else fails." He handed it to Mohammad.

The Prophet gasped and took the object. Holding the bejeweled and intricately tooled leather scabbard in one hand, with the other he drew out a curved sword. It was most wicked looking weapon he had ever seen. The blade was shiny and beaten to razor sharpness. His hand fit perfectly inside the guard, grip, and pommel. He hefted it once or twice. It had an admirable balance. "Milord!" he exclaimed. "What workmanship! What is it called?"

"It is a scimitar," answered Gabriel, ignoring the open-mouthed amazement of the scribe, to whom the weapon had appeared miraculously in Mohammad's hands without cause. "It is a better tool for conversion than the spears and flat swords your companions carry." He paused and looked sly. "What does its form remind you of, Mohammad?"

The Prophet's sight was fixed on the gleaming metal. His mind was dazzled. He shook his head.

"Allah is the Moon God, and that is the shape of the quarter moon. Henceforth, that will be your symbol, and your pulpit, so to speak. Sew that symbol to your banners. Now, get to work! Pack up everything here and move to Medina! There you may plot without distraction." With that, the Angel Gabriel said, "ma'a as-salaama," and went poof.

"Thank Allah for me," said Mohammad to the empty air.

So, Sura 53:19-20 were emended to deny the reality of Allah's daughters. These are verses 21-22.

Of course, this embarrassing and compromising episode was reported over a century after Mohammad's alleged death (his existence being alleged anyway) by Ibn Ishaq and al-Tabari. They had cell phone camera video evidence of the confrontation and correction – recorded by an anonymous witness, who may have been Baal – but that evidence was lost during the turmoil of the Islamic conquest of the Arabian Peninsula.

As everyone knows, Islam was so far ahead of its time. Lost also are volumes on quantum mechanics, heart transplants, the discovery of Uranus and Neptune, various heliocentric theories, a tantalizing treatise on electricity, a dissertation on agricultural irrigation, not to mention the entire *oeuvre* of Abdul ibn-Knish, including his Córdoban comedies. Western scholars argue that ibn-Knish was the Noël Coward of his day, to judge by the pitifully few fragments of his plays that are preserved in the Vatican Library. It is thought by experts that the Angel Samantha served as ibn-Knish's muse, going by the name of Elvira.

In the Unexpurgated *Koran*, only one copy of which has survived and which is secured in a booby-trapped vault deep beneath the Vatican, another scholar relates that it was the Angel Samantha who whispered the untruths into Mohammad's ear about Allah's daughters. In this rare, early copy of the *Koran*, Suras 53 through 57 have been nicknamed the "Henpecked Allah Verses."

The Angel Samantha was in due course unceremoniously chucked out of Paradise by Allah, once he learned of her betrayal and her role in advising Mohammad behind Gabriel's back. As she plummeted to the flaming nether regions in a burqa, she balled up a fist, punched a hole through it, and shouted back, "Oh, who wants to sit at your stinking feet forever singing your praises, you megalomaniac!" It is reputed that she formed a liaison with Shayton and assisted him over the millennia in spurring hostile and often bloody divisions among Muslims. It was, underground scholars aver, she who enticed many Muslims to part from the Sunnis and become Shi'ites, whose original name was "She's It!" It was quite a radical career change.

The End

*   *   *

Of course, most of the *Korans* that are regularly burned by Muslims are those containing the uncorrected Sura 53 and other shocking and prurient chapters that were simply edited out of standard, general circulation *Korans* over the centuries by conscientious Islamic scholars. It explains much, such as why most Muslims are a humorless lot and super-sensitive to any criticism. Muslims are a most repressed people. And the *Korans* with the corrected Sura 53 underscore Islam's inherent and wholly creditable misogyny, not to mention the scale of its troubling and murderous psychosis.

March 2012

Edward Cline

Who's Destroying Western Civilization?

In his "An Explanatory Memorandum on the General Strategic Goal for the Brotherhood in North America," Muslim Brotherhood member Mohamed Akram wrote:

> Enablement of Islam in North America, meaning: establishing an effective and stable Islamic Movement led by the Muslim Brotherhood which adopts Muslims' causes domestically and globally, and which works to expand the observant Muslim base, aims at unifying and directing Muslims' efforts, presents Islam as a civilization alternative, and supports the global Islamic state, wherever it is.

> The process of settlement is a "Civilization-Jihadist Process" with all the word means. The Ikhwan must understand that their work in America is a kind of grand Jihad in eliminating and destroying the Western civilization from within and "sabotaging" its miserable house by their hands and the hands of the believers so that it is eliminated and God's religion is made victorious over all other religions.

Steve Emerson of the Investigative Project on Terrorism notes:

> This May 1991 memo was written by Mohamed Akram, a.k.a. Mohamed Adlouni, for the Shura Council of the Muslim Brotherhood. In the introductory letter, Akram referenced a "long-term plan...approved and adopted" by the Shura Council in 1987 and proposed this memo as a supplement to that plan and requested that the memo be added to the agenda for an upcoming Council meeting. Appended to the document is a list of all Muslim Brotherhood organizations in North America as of 1991.

There are many fine, important, and informative essays and books on just how antithetical Islam is to Western values – to individualism, to private property, to freedom of speech – and on just how insidious and anti-life it is. But few are the books and essays on why Islam seems to be making progress in its "grand jihad" against the West.

Who or what is actually destroying Western Civilization from within? The Islamists? Or the West? What contributes to the Islamists' hubris, what encourages them and instills them with confidence that they can "conquer"

87

the West, and especially the United States. Whose "hands" are working together with those of the "believers" to bring down Western civilization and establish Sharia law here and everywhere?

Islam would be as impotent as Scientology, or of a cult that ascribed mystical powers to pyramids or a diet of bottles of Shaklee vitamins. Is Islam imbued with some inexorable and ineluctable power to conquer the West?
One thing is that Islamists are shrewd enough to exploit the corrosive policies of cultural relativism, multiculturalism, the commitment to "diversity," indiscriminate "tolerance," subjectivism, and a host of other policies that assault or negate reason and all standards of measurement of value, superiority and inferiority. Islam is as bankrupt of formal philosophy as is the culture it is "sabotaging." The intelligence exhibited by Islamists is merely a feral, predatory intelligence. Islam allows no other kind. Islam does not permit independent thought, only agreement with arbitrary assertions.

A wolf may be predatory, but that is how it is programmed by nature. It has no choice in the matter. A Muslim is a man imbued with volition and the capacity for choice; he chooses to limit himself to an ideology that permits him to be merely feral and predatory and submissive. His mind merely detects his enemy's weaknesses and vulnerabilities – weaknesses and vulnerabilities that are as self-inflicted as choosing to be a Muslim – and plots to exploit them.

Those weaknesses and vulnerabilities are the West's policies, noted above. And what are the philosophical foundations of those policies? The reigning philosophy is that one cannot know anything, either for certain or at all, that all values are relative, or subjective, that reality is whatever one wishes it to be. On one or more of those premises, there are no absolutes that a defender of the West can repair to or uphold.

The Seattle Times reprinted an Associated Press item about a Saudi religious figure warning Muslims and non-Muslims to "respect" the Muslim month of Ramadan.

> Saudi authorities warned non-Muslim expatriates on Friday, the first day of Ramadan, not to eat, drink, or smoke in public until the end of the Muslim holy month's sunrise-to-sunset fast - or face expulsion.... The prince newly appointed to handle most aspects of law enforcement is known as a strict adherent to religious rules.

Prince Ahmed bin Abdulaziz was governor of the holy city of
Mecca before becoming Interior Minister.

I do not think very many people realize that showing respect and deference
to Muslim practices and sensitivities outside of Muslim countries is a form
of submission to Islam, regardless of the Islamic holiday or the day of the
year. This is especially true of those who know little about Islam and have
not grasped the implications of granting such respect. They are more
concerned with not wanting to hurt Muslim "feelings" than they are with
the content of those feelings.

According to the cultural relativism most Westerners are indoctrinated
with today, Muslim "feelings" are sacrosanct and not to be troubled or
offended. "Feelings," they are taught, are a tool of cognition, in themselves
and in Muslims, so to offend Muslim feelings is to question a Muslim's
world view, and a Muslim's world view – in which Allah owns everything
and everyone and Mohammad was his prophet – is just as good as anyone
else's. Showing disrespect for a Muslim's feelings implies that one's own
feelings are somehow superior to his. So a Muslim's feelings must be
respected.

There is no such thing as an absolute, goes the line, only perceptions of
things filtered by a person's bias or prepossession or taste, and molded by
one's culture, and so a Muslim's perceptions are just as valid as anyone
else's. These perceptions cannot be judged because there are no absolutes
by which to judge them. A host of Western philosophers have said so,
such as Descartes and Kant and Hegel, and vetted by thinkers such as
William James, Sartre, and John Dewey and many lesser lights.

Who knows, ask the *dhimmis-by-default* when they bother to ponder the
question, and who perhaps have never heard of Hegel or Kant or
Descartes, Muslims might be right. "Muslims feel, therefore they exist," is
how they might parody Descartes and characterize the Islamic mindset, if
they dared to carry the thought to that point. Who is any non-Muslim to
judge a Muslim, or what a Muslim believes? While what works for
Muslims may not work for non-Muslims, that's just a matter of feeling and
up-bringing. It just isn't practical to offend a Muslim's feelings. Who can
blame them for rioting and killing when the cultures Muslims immigrate to
are hostile to their confidence that theirs is the only true religion and that
are not natural environments in which to practice their creed? It is
irrelevant that Islam is antithetical and hostile to the notion of individual
rights. Muslims must be cut some slack, and be accommodated whenever
possible. Civilizational clashes must be avoided. How else can non-

Muslims prove they are tolerant and civilized except by respecting
Muslims on bent knee and with bowed head?
The rumors that Islam is "eliminating" Western civilization by
"sabotaging" it from within it are only half true. Thanks to a philosophy of
unreason, promulgated by Western thinkers and taught in the best schools
in the West over the course of two centuries, Western civilization is
destroying itself "by its own hand." And the United States is proving to be
very, very accommodating. It has even elected an unbroken succession of
Accommodators-in-Chief, beginning with the Peanut Farmer.

That Brotherhood fellow Mohamed Akram was on to something.

Minnesota Representative Michele Bachmann dared to call for an
investigation of Muslims in the federal government, especially of Muslims
closely or remotely connected to the Muslim Brotherhood. She was
immediately attacked by the "gangster government" from all quarters,
including that of the mainstream media.

> Rep. Michele Bachmann says the Muslim Brotherhood, the
> international Islamist movement that recently came to power in
> Egypt, has made "deep penetration" within the U.S. government,
> and she wants an investigation of its influence within five federal
> agencies.
>
> The Muslim Brotherhood, perhaps the world's most influential
> Islamist organization, has long sought to unite traditional Islam
> with modern democracy in Middle Eastern nations. Its global
> influence further increased when one of its candidates, Mohamed
> Morsi, was declared winner of Egypt's 2012 presidential election.
> But Bachmann, R-Stillwater, and four other members of Congress
> see the Muslim Brotherhood as a domestic threat.
>
> The lawmakers singled out the movement last month in letters to
> federal defense, diplomatic, intelligence and law-enforcement
> agencies, requesting investigations into whether — and through
> whom — the Muslim Brotherhood is exerting influence within
> President Barack Obama's administration.
>
> Bachmann, who serves on the House Permanent Select Committee
> on Intelligence, ratcheted up the rhetoric in an interview last
> month with radio host Sandy Rios.

90

"It appears that there has been deep penetration in the halls of our United States government by the Muslim Brotherhood," Bachmann said. "It appears that there are individuals who are associated with the Muslim Brotherhood who have positions, very sensitive positions, in our Department of Justice, our Department of Homeland Security, potentially even in the National Intelligence Agency."

One of those individuals is Huma Abedin. Abedin is Secretary of State Hillary Clinton's long-time personal advisor, especially on things Islamic.

Robert Spencer wrote about the controversy:

> Congresswoman Michele Bachmann (R-MN) is at the center of a firestorm over her request that the State, Homeland Security, Defense and Justice Departments, investigate potential "policies and activities that appear to be the result of influence operations conducted by individuals and organizations associated with the Muslim Brotherhood." This is an entirely legitimate call, as Bachmann abundantly illustrated in a 16-page letter to Muslim Congressman Keith Ellison (D-MN), laying out the reasons for her concerns. Yet even Senator John McCain (R-AZ), who should know better, has upbraided Bachmann, criticizing her for including Hillary Clinton's top aide, Huma Abedin, among those she noted for having Brotherhood ties.

The Seattle Times also ran an editorial against Bachmann that concludes with a statement that should win the Politically Clueless Award for 2012:

> While Abedin's 20 years of public service should save her reputation from assaults by an unthinking zealot who once equated the national debt to the Holocaust, Bachmann's latest actions deserve the same censure in Congress that Joseph McCarthy received for his witch hunt for Communists 60 years ago.

Not knowing or evading the fact that men dedicated to communism and totalitarianism are now running the government? This is an instance of either an appalling ignorance of history, or a willful evasion of the facts. But whichever diagnosis is correct, it underscores a critical disconnection from reality. In the first instance, it represents ignorance of reality; in the second, a willful dislike of reality. Mental lethargy can help to explain the first; mental evasion, the second (and evasion does require mental effort).

Leonard Peikoff, in his seminal, 1967 essay, "The Analytic-Synthetic Dichotomy" in the *Introduction to Objectivist Epistemology* by Ayn Rand*, explains this disconnection. After demonstrating the false distinction between "logical" and "empirical" arguments about ice sinking in water, he writes:

> This argument confuses Walt Disney with metaphysics. That a man can project an image or draw an animated cartoon at variance with the facts of reality, does not alter the facts….An image of ice sinking in water does not alter the nature of ice [that it floats in water]; it does not constitute evidence that it is possible for ice to sink in water. It is evidence only of man's capacity to engage in fantasy. Fantasy is not a form of cognition.

"Logically," Huma Abedin has been in government service since 1996 (beginning with the Clinton administration) and so must be a loyal American and not dedicated to the overthrow or transformation of the government into a totalitarian, Islamic one. "Empirically," she cannot be a Muslim Brotherhood operative because she has not been seen wearing a suicide vest or caught using a secret decoder ring or photographed using an Islamic drop box to deposit classified government documents. Besides, she is a snappy dresser, something most Muslim women are not. Ergo, it is unconscionable to accuse her of having dangerous and sympathetic Islamic associations.

Peikoff continues:

> Further: the fact that man possesses the capacity to fantasize does not mean that the opposite of demonstrated truths is "imaginable" or "conceivable." In a serious, epistemological sense of the word, a man *cannot* conceive the opposite of a proposition he knows to be true (as apart from propositions dealing with man-made facts). If a proposition asserting a metaphysical fact has been demonstrated to be true, this means that that fact has been demonstrated to be inherent in the identities of the entities in question, and that any alternative to it would require the existence of a contradiction.

> *Only ignorance or evasion can enable a man to attempt to project such an alternative.* If a man does not know that a certain fact has been demonstrated, he will not know that its denial involves a contradiction. If a man does know it, but evades the knowledge and drops his full cognitive context, there is no limit to what he

92

can pretend to conceive. But what one can project by means of ignorance or evasion, is philosophically irrelevant. It does not constitute a basis for instituting two separate categories of possibility. (p. 116, *Italics* mine)

The illegitimate possibilities? According to Senator John McCain, Speaker of the House John Boehner, the MSM, and all those other *dhimmis-by-default*, Huma Abedin, a Muslim, may or may not be an influence on Obama's foreign policy via Hillary Clinton, regardless of her association or her family's association with an organization dedicated to conquering America and establishing totalitarian rule. As Robert Spencer relates, they are asking Bachmann for evidence *now* of an investigation that has not been undertaken by those responsible it. That is the "logical" position.

The "empirical" position is: So what if she's a Muslim? She's a nice, hard-working person.

The Western hands helping the hands of Islamic believers to "sabotage" the miserable house of Western civilization are many, small, and mean. Their owners' minds are either permanently lost in a Fantasy Land divorced from reality, or so myopically concrete-bound that they are in pathetic need of the corrective lenses of a rational epistemology.

Ignorant or evasive, together their minds constitute a "brotherhood" of another kind.

Introduction to Objectivist Epistemology by Ayn Rand. (1966, 1967, 1979) Eds. Harry Binswanger and Leonard Peikoff. New York: Meridian-Penguin. Second Edition, 1990. 314 pp.

July 2012

Natural Allies Against Liberty

Just as the Witch Doctor is impotent without Attila, so Attila is impotent without the Witch Doctor; neither can make his power last without the other.*

I am for freedom of religion and against all maneuvers to bring about a legal ascendancy of one sect over another.**

In all ages, hypocrites, called priests, have put crowns upon the heads of thieves, called kings.***

The United States Conference of Catholic Bishops lent its endorsement to the 2,000+ page health care bill passed by the House last week (H.R. 3962), when Speaker of the House Nancy Pelosi and her arm-twisting cohorts persuaded others to okay the Stupak-Pitts Amendment. The amendment would prohibit insurance companies from including coverage for federally-subsidized abortions in their health plans, or so restrict them that it would not encourage any insurance company to include an abortion a covered medical procedure.

The amendment, which passed by a vote of 240 to 194, would be included in the so-called "public option" of the legislation. The term "public option," however, is a deceptive misnomer. There is nothing "public" about it. It would place a government bureaucrat in between an insurer and the insured. It should be called the "bureaucratic option."

What has not been paid much attention is the fact that an organization of Catholic clergy has prevailed upon a nominally secular government to impose its religious dogma -- that fetuses are persons from the moment of conception -- on the rest of the country, in the face of opposition by several other religious groups, including one called Catholics for Choice. Of course, few in Congress, least of all Pelosi and her mandating munchkins and trolls, care to think of the First Amendment of the Constitution or even to give it serious credence, or perhaps devote two seconds of consideration of it in their power-obsessed minds. The words in that amendment are simple, clear and brief. It states that:

> "Congress shall make no law respecting an establishment of religion, or prohibiting the free exercise thereof..."

The establishment clause prohibits Congress from creating a state religion, while the free exercise clause bars Congress from granting "most-favored religion" status to any religion at the expense of or over another (that is, while not literally creating a state religion).

Balance that against the mammoth health care bill with its millions of words. The question, however, is: Can the endorsement of the anti-abortion provision by the bishops, together with the concession by Pelosi (also a Catholic) and her allies in response to the peevish machinations of Stupak and his allies, be construed as the establishment of a religion?

Actually, no. But it hovers close to it. In fact, the American Catholic Church is a major recipient of federal funds. Its collection basket overflows with taxpayer money. It should come as no surprise that the bishops could exert such extraordinary influence on a nominally secular Congress. Politico reports:

> With well over half of their revenue coming from the government, it is safe to say that Catholic hospitals survive on government funding as well as contributions from private sources....Catholic Charities, the domestic direct service arm of the bishops, also depends on state and federal dollars. Sixty-seven percent of Catholic Charities' income comes from government funding. That represents over $2.6 billion in 2008 — an amount that is more than three times as large as the next largest charitable recipient of federal funds, the YMCA. Just as Catholic hospitals do, Catholic Charities receives enormous quantities of government dollars while abiding by existing constitutional and statutory requirements that prevent government sponsorship of religion.

How the Stupak-Pitts Amendment to the health care bill came to be an issue is completely consistent with the character of the bill itself. In a move that smacks of extortion of extortionists. Bart Stupak, a Michigan Democrat (and Catholic) who sponsored the amendment, together with Pennsylvania Republican representative Joseph Pitts (an evangelical Christian), promised that they and other Democrats and Republicans would block passage of the bill if it permitted the federal subsidy of abortions in conjunction with the bill's insurance coverage. Joining them in that maneuver were Democratic Representatives Ike Skelton of Missouri, John Tanner and Lincoln Davis of Tennessee, and Dan Boren of Oklahoma.

They were apparently moved to initiate that maneuver by the first bishops' letter, dated October 10, in which, among other things, the bishops demanded that the bill:

> Exclude mandated coverage for abortion, and incorporate longstanding policies against abortion funding and in favor of conscience rights. No one should be required to pay for or participate in abortion. It is essential that the legislation clearly apply to this new program longstanding and widely supported federal restrictions on abortion funding and mandates, and protections for rights of conscience. No current bill meets this test.

Otherwise, the bishops warned:

> If final legislation does not meet our principles, we will have no choice but to oppose the bill. We remain committed to working with the Administration, Congressional leadership, and our allies to produce final health reform legislation that will reflect our principles.

Once the amendment had passed, however, the bishops wrote the House:

> We are very pleased that the House leadership has agreed to allow the essential Stupak-Pitts-Kaptur-Dahlkemper-Lipinski-Smith Amendment to be considered by the House. This amendment will add to the Affordable Health Care for America Act (H.R. 3962) crucial provisions that maintain the current protections against abortion funding and mandates. Specifically, it will achieve our objective of applying the provisions of the Hyde amendment to the public health plan and on the affordability credits in the exchanges called for in the legislation.
>
> Passing this amendment allows the House to meet our criteria of preserving the existing protections against abortion funding in the new legislation. It also would fulfill President Obama's commitment in this area. Most importantly, it will ensure that no government funds will be used for abortion or health plans which include abortion. It is a major step forward.

In the bishops' first letter there is no reference to or mention of the premise that abortion is immoral, or that fetuses are "persons" with "rights." Those are merely covered by the disingenuous phrases, "rights of conscience" and "our principles." What "rights" and what "principles"? As Ayn Rand would retort: Blank-out. In the second, congratulatory letter, the bishops felt they no longer needed to mention "rights" or "principles." They were only too happy to pat the Stupak syndicate on the back.

Catholics and their clergy are not the only religious groups that oppose abortion on moral grounds. There are secular opponents, as well. The question, then, is not whether there are any provable grounds to such a position, but whether or not such an idea, grounded on mere emotionalist assertions, has any business influencing *any* legislation.

In both of the bishops' letters, the premise is not spoken, revealed, or even implied. It has been merely incorporated into the arid language of the bill concerning federal funding of abortions and insurance coverage.

In an apparent digression here, it would be apropos to quote Ayn Rand from her 1964 Playboy interview. Asked about her alleged remark about the cross being a symbol of torture, she replied:

> To begin with, I never said that. It's not my style....What is correct is that I do regard the cross as the symbol of the sacrifice of the ideal to the nonideal. Isn't that what it does mean? Christ, in terms of the Christian philosophy, is the human ideal. He personifies that which men should strive to emulate. Yet, according to the Christian mythology, he died on the cross not for his own sins but for the sins of the nonideal people. In other words, a man of perfect virtue was sacrificed for men who are vicious and who are expected or supposed to accept that sacrifice. If I were a Christian, nothing could make me more indignant than that: the notion of sacrificing the ideal to the non-ideal, or virtue to vice. And it is in the name of that symbol that men are asked to sacrifice themselves for their inferiors. That is precisely how the symbolism is used. That is torture.

What is the bishops' premise? What is their principle? Just as environmentalists expect man to sacrifice his well-being, standard of living, longevity, and happiness in the name of "preserving" the earth or the climate or polar bears or weeds, women are specifically expected to be virtuous by sacrificing their lives and happiness for the sake of a *non-ideal*, that is, for the sake of a fetus, or a *non-person*.

So it is logical that the bishops would endorse the entire, sacrifice-through-coercion health care legislation. It is doubtful that they actually believe in the nonsense that fetuses have "rights." They *know*, in the dark, unexamined cores of their souls, that the bill is a prescription for slavery and sacrifice to all the "non-ideal" men and women in the country. They are the Witch Doctors working hand-in-hand with the Attilas. Virtue comes from the point of a gun. They pose as "pro-life," when, in fact, they are *anti-life*.

Had the bishops not intervened and played politics with the House sponsors and advocates of the health care bill, the provisions that cover insurance-covered abortions would probably have remained untouched. This is aside from the issue that the whole bill virtually appropriates Americans' bodies and wealth for the sake of the poor, the uninsured, illegal immigrants -- and fetuses. The bishops are indifferent to the fact that the bill lays the groundwork for totalitarianism in this country. They are oblivious to the virtual enslavement of the medical profession. Their "rights of conscience" and "principles" trump those of all other Americans.

The bishops are not only *anti-choice* in the matter of abortion, but *anti-choice* in the most fundamental sense of individual rights. The Bill of Rights means as little to them as it does to most members of Congress. They are the natural allies of the totalitarians in the House and Senate.

*"For the New Intellectual," in *For the New Intellectual: The Philosophy of Ayn Rand.* New York: Signet, 1961, p. 23.

**Thomas Jefferson, letter to Elbridge Gerry, January 26, 1799. From Gorton Carruth and Eugene Ehrlich, eds., *The Harper Book of American Quotations*, New York: Harper & Row, 1988, p. 499.

***Robert G. Ingersoll, 1833-1899, *Prose Poems and Selections*, 1884. From Daniel B. Baker, ed., Political Quotations, Detroit: Gale Research, Inc., 1990, p. 190.

November 2009

Edward Cline

The Sticky Wickets of "Radical" Islam

In a 1983 all-star pirate comedy, *Yellowbeard*, basically an expensively sewn grab bag of sight gags, one-liners, and pratfalls, there is one scene in which most of the principal characters, in search of Yellowbeard's treasure, form a kind of conga line on a beach, crawling on their hands and knees, following cryptically written directions on a piece of paper that may lead them to the buried chest. As a yawner, it was a low point in a sequence of low points. We were not amused.

I was reminded of that scene while reading another low point of political enquiry, the British Home Affairs Committee report, *The Roots of Violent Radicalisation.* In search of the reasons why British-born Muslims and immigrant Muslims turn to terrorism, this lengthy report asks many questions but answers none, tip-toeing as it does around the central ideological content of Islam that is at radical (and violent) variance with Western values, and could be characterized as a conga line of magnifying class-equipped twits examining every little grain of sand and pebble and tide-swept debris in search of those answers. The committee was chaired by a Muslim, Member for Leicester, Keith Vaz, a scandal-soaked politician who, among his many other offenses, in 1989 lead thousands of Muslims in a demonstration to demand the banning of Salman Rushdie's *The Satanic Verses.*

The Home Affairs Committee report differs little from what passes for Congressional studies of the same subject (except for the Peter King hearings), which have for over a decade bent over backwards to identify the roots of Islamic jihad but not mention or incriminate Muslims or Islam itself.

Here are some randomly selected excerpts from the report that treat "violent extremist" Muslims as victims or put-upon, passive, and helpless Islamic receptors of "extremism":

> The empirical evidence base on what factors make an individual more vulnerable to Al Qa'ida-influenced violent extremism is weak. Even less is known about why certain individuals resort to violence, when other individuals from the same community, with similar experiences, do not become involved in violent activity.

> We suspect that violent radicalisation is declining within the Muslim community. There may be growing support for nonviolent

99

extremism, fed by feelings of alienation, and while this may not lead to a specific terrorist threat or be a staging post for violent extremism, it is nevertheless a major challenge for society in general and for the police in particular.

One of the few clear conclusions we were able to draw about the drivers of radicalisation is that a sense of grievance is key to the process. Addressing perceptions of Islamophobia, and demonstrating that the British state is not antithetical to Islam, should constitute a main focus of the part of the Prevent Strategy which is designed to counter the ideology feeding violent radicalisation.

The Government notes in the Prevent Strategy that individuals "who distrust Parliament" are at particular risk of violent radicalisation. This appeared to be borne out in our inquiry, both in terms of Islamist and extreme far-right- radicalisation.

However, the Committee report concludes, not so startlingly and in conformance with calls in the U.S. to adopt the same policy:

The Committee concludes that the internet is one of the most significant vehicles for promoting violent radicalism - more so than prisons, universities or places of worship, although direct, personal contact with radicals is in many cases also a significant factor. Witnesses told the Committee that the internet played a part in most, if not all, cases of violent radicalisation.

Although there are statutory powers under the Terrorism Act 2006 for law enforcement agencies to order unlawful material to be removed from the internet, the Committee recommends that internet service providers themselves should be more active in monitoring the material they host, with appropriate guidance, advice and support from the Government. The Government should work with internet providers to develop a code of practice for the removal of material which promotes violent extremism.

Let us put some well-deserved words in the Committee's collective mouth.

Where do those "radicals" come from? From the realm of "disaffection"? From the nursery of "alienation"? From the islands of "grievance"? We really can't reach any definite conclusions, because, after all, Islam is a "religion of peace" and to say otherwise will only compound feelings of alienation and contribute to the grievance racket, err, that is to say, such a careless and hurtful assertion would solicit more complaints from the aggrieved. If there is any disaffection or alienation out there, it's all the fault of British society and its Western values.

And we mustn't place much importance on prisons, mosques, and universities as incubators of "radicalism" – we've done our best not to look, or pay attention to the percentage of prisoners who are Muslim or who convert to Islam, or to record the hateful rantings of Muslim clerics in places of worship, or the clotting of Muslim students on university campuses and their participation in "Islam will Dominate Britain" rallies.

Rather, we should focus our attention on the Internet.

Of this we are certain: the Internet, after all, is an efficient facilitator of communication among terrorists and would-be terrorists and other "extremists," including those who oppose the Islamization of Britain. The government must monitor Internet traffic and sites more effectively than it does at the present, and persuade providers and ISP owners to do a better job of self-policing. We are particularly interested in sites that promote or invite "hate speech" and other modes of illegal expression. We would like to see these vanish from the Internet just to save us all a spot of bother.

Of course, any legislation introduced in the House that would adopt our recommendations would invite opposition from those concerned about freedom of speech and the like, but we are confident that these objections can be circumvented without hurting anyone's feelings. It has been done before.

At the moment, however, budgetary constraints prohibit Her Majesty's government from emulating the American Department of Homeland Security and monitoring every bit of Internet usage and red-flagging every suspicious word and image. Muslims are a minority in Britain (at the moment), and we mustn't leave them feeling left out of the political process (we discount the number of Muslims in the Commons and those who have been elevated to the Peerage, they're a minority, too, and we don't feel that the Muslim community are satisfied with such "tokenism").

The Home Affairs Committee regret not having been able to reach any definitive conclusions, except on the role of the Internet. We will convene again soon and brandish our new, improved magnifying glasses to better and more thoroughly examine how the Internet contributes to extremism and radicalisation, and discuss how best to solve these sticky wickets.

We have one standing rule, however, which will go far in our fair and disinterested deliberations: No one will be allowed to quote Winston Churchill on the nature of Islam and the character of Muslims. Some members of the Committee find his statements violently offensive. Particularly Mr. Vaz.

February 2012

The "Peaceful" *Koran*'s Violent Verses

For doubters, scoffers, fence-sitters, shirkers, and others who claim that Islamophobes make mountains out of molehills about Islam and its compulsory *jihad* against the West and non-Muslims, offered here is a short selection of verses from the *Koran* (*Qur'an*) and the *Hadith* that should disabuse them of the nature and ends of Islam. To cite these and a multitude of similar verses, claim Islamists of the clerical and violent kind, is to defame Islam, and to engage in blasphemy and misrepresentation.

Go figure. Imagine that one cited passages from Adolf Hitler's *Mein Kampf* that ranted against Jews and other racial or religious groups, and then was charged with misrepresenting and defaming Nazism. *Mein Kampf,* by the way, is a continual best-seller in the Mideast. It was not for nothing that Geert Wilders, the Dutch politician who has been marked for death by a *fatwa* for "blaspheming" Islam, similar to that issued on Salman Rushdie for *The Satanic Verses,* claimed that the *Koran* is the Islamic *Mein Kampf.* And, because *Mein Kampf* is a popular title with Muslims, one must wonder why they would object to the comparison.

Enjoy – and learn.

Qur'an 5:3
This day have I perfected your religion for you and completed My favor upon you and have chosen for you Islam as your religion.

Qur'an 54:17
And We have indeed made the Qur'an easy to understand and remember, then is there any that will remember (or receive admonition)?

Qur'an 9:88
The Messenger and those who believe with him, strive hard and fight with their wealth and lives in Allah's Cause.

Qur'an 9:5
Fight and kill the disbelievers wherever you find them, take them captive, harass them, lie in wait and ambush them using every stratagem of war.

Qur'an 9:112
The Believers fight in Allah's Cause, they slay and are slain, kill and are killed.

Qur'an 9:29
Fight those who do not believe until they all surrender, paying the protective tax in submission.

Ishaq:325 "Muslims, fight in Allah's Cause. Stand firm and you will prosper. Help the Prophet, obey him, give him your allegiance, and your religion will be victorious."

Qur'an:8:39 "Fight them until all opposition ends and all submit to Allah."

Qur'an:8:39 "So fight them until there is no more Fitnah (disbelief [non-Muslims]) and all submit to the religion of Allah alone (in the whole world)."

Ishaq:324 "He said, 'Fight them so that there is no more rebellion, and religion, all of it, is for Allah only. Allah must have no rivals.'"

Qur'an:9:14 "Fight them and Allah will punish them by your hands, lay them low, and cover them with shame. He will help you over them."

Ishaq:300 "I am fighting in Allah's service. This is piety and a good deed. In Allah's war I do not fear as others should. For this fighting is righteous, true, and good."

Ishaq:587 "Our onslaught will not be a weak faltering affair. We shall fight as long as we live. We will fight until you turn to Islam, humbly seeking refuge. We will fight not caring whom we meet. We will fight whether we destroy ancient holdings or newly gotten gains. We have mutilated every opponent. We have driven them violently before us at the command of Allah and Islam. We will fight until our religion is established. And we will plunder them, for they must suffer disgrace."

Qur'an:8:65 "O Prophet, urge the faithful to fight. If there are twenty among you with determination they will vanquish two hundred; if there are a hundred then they will slaughter a thousand unbelievers, for the infidels are a people devoid of understanding."

Ishaq:326 "Prophet exhort the believers to fight. If there are twenty good fighters they will defeat two hundred for they are a senseless people. They do not fight with good intentions nor for truth."

Hadith, Sahih Bukhari:V4B52N63 "A man whose face was covered with an iron mask came to the Prophet and said, 'Allah's Apostle! Shall I fight or embrace Islam first?' The Prophet said, 'Embrace Islam first and then fight.' So he embraced Islam, and was martyred. Allah's Apostle said, 'A Little work, but a great reward.'"

Bukhari:V4B53N386 "Our Prophet, the Messenger of our Lord, ordered us to fight you till you worship Allah alone or pay us the Jizyah tribute tax in submission. Our Prophet has informed us that our Lord says: 'Whoever amongst us is killed as a martyr shall go to Paradise to lead such a luxurious life as he has never seen, and whoever survives shall become your master.'"

Hadith, Sahih Muslim:C34B20N4668 "The Messenger said: 'Anybody who equips a warrior going to fight in the Way of Allah is like one who actually fights. And anybody who looks after his family in his absence is also like one who actually fights."

Qur'an:9:38 "Believers, what is the matter with you, that when you are asked to go forth and fight in Allah's Cause you cling to the earth? Do you prefer the life of this world to the Hereafter? Unless you go forth, He will afflict and punish you with a painful doom, and put others in your place."

Qur'an:9:123 "Fight the unbelievers around you, and let them find harshness in you."

Qur'an:8:72 "Those who accepted Islam and left their homes to fight in Allah's Cause with their possessions and persons, and those who gave (them) asylum, aid, and shelter, those who harbored them - these are allies of one another. You are not responsible for protecting those who embraced Islam but did not leave their homes [to fight] until they do so." [Another translation reads:] "You are only called to protect Muslims who fight."

Muslim:C9B1N31 "I have been commanded to fight against people till they testify to the fact that there is no god but Allah, and believe in me (that) I am the Messenger and in all that I have brought."

Bukhari:V9B84N59 "Whoever says this will save his property and life from me.'"

Qur'an:8:73 "The unbelieving infidels are allies. Unless you (Muslims) aid each other (fighting as one united block to make Allah's religion victorious), there will be confusion and mischief. Those who accepted Islam, left their homes to fight in Allah's Cause (al-Jihad), as well as those who give them asylum, shelter, and aid - these are (all) Believers: for them is pardon and bountiful provision (in Paradise)."

Tabari IX:69 "Arabs are the most noble people in lineage, the most prominent, and the best in deeds. We were the first to respond to the call of the Prophet. We are Allah's helpers and the viziers of His Messenger. We fight people until they believe in Allah. He who believes in Allah and His Messenger has protected his life and possessions from us. As for one who disbelieves, we will fight him forever in the Cause of Allah. Killing him is a small matter to us."

Qur'an:48:16 "Say (Muhammad) to the wandering desert Arabs who lagged behind: 'You shall be invited to fight against a people given to war with mighty prowess. You shall fight them until they surrender and submit. If you obey, Allah will grant you a reward, but if you turn back, as you did before, He will punish you with a grievous torture."

Qur'an:48:22 "If the unbelieving infidels fight against you, they will retreat. (Such has been) the practice (approved) of Allah in the past: no change will you find in the ways of Allah."

Qur'an:47:4 "When you clash with the unbelieving Infidels in battle (fighting Jihad in Allah's Cause), smite their necks until you overpower them, killing and wounding many of them. At length, when you have thoroughly subdued them, bind them firmly, making (them) captives. Thereafter either generosity or ransom (them based upon what benefits Islam) until the war lays down its burdens. Thus are you commanded by Allah to continue carrying out Jihad against the unbelieving infidels until they submit to Islam."

Qur'an:47:31 "And We shall try you until We know those among you who are the fighters."

Tabari VI:138 "Those present at the oath of Aqabah had sworn an allegiance to Muhammad. It was a pledge of war against all men. Allah had permitted fighting."

Tabari VI:139 "Allah had given his Messenger permission to fight by revealing the verse 'And fight them until persecution is no more, and religion is all for Allah.'"

Qur'an:9:19 "Do you make the giving of drink to pilgrims, or the maintenance of the Mosque, equal to those who fight in the Cause of Allah? They are not comparable in the sight of Allah. Those who believe, and left their homes, striving with might, fighting in Allah's Cause with their goods and their lives, have the highest rank in the sight of Allah."

Ishaq:550 "The Muslims met them with their swords. They cut through many arms and skulls. Only confused cries and groans could be heard over our battle roars and snarling."

Qur'an:5:94 "Believers, Allah will make a test for you in the form of a little game in which you reach out for your lances. Any who fails this test will have a grievous punishment."

Ishaq:578 "Crushing the heads of the infidels and splitting their skulls with sharp swords, we continually thrust and cut at the enemy. Blood gushed from their deep wounds as the battle wore them down. We conquered bearing the Prophet's fluttering war banner. Our cavalry was submerged in rising dust, and our spears quivered, but by us the Prophet gained victory."

Tabari IX:22 "The Prophet continued to besiege the town, fighting them bitterly."

Tabari IX:25 "By Allah, I did not come to fight for nothing. I wanted a victory over Ta'if so that I might obtain a slave girl from them and make her pregnant."

Tabari IX:82 "The Messenger sent Khalid with an army of 400 to Harith [a South Arabian tribe] and ordered him to invite them to Islam for three days before he fought them. If they were to respond and submit, he was to teach them the Book of Allah, the Sunnah of His Prophet, and the requirements of Islam. If they should decline, then he was to fight them."

Tabari IX:88 "Abdallah Azdi came to the Messenger, embraced Islam, and became a good Muslim. Allah's Apostle invested Azdi with the authority over those who had surrendered and ordered him to fight the infidels from the tribes of Yemen. Azdi left with an army by the Messenger's command. The Muslims besieged them for a month. Then they withdrew, setting a trap. When the Yemenites went in pursuit, Azdi was able to inflict a heavy loss on them."

Ishaq:530 "Get out of his way, you infidel unbelievers. Every good thing goes with the Apostle. Lord, I believe in his word. We will fight you about its interpretations as we have fought you about its revelation with strokes that will remove heads from shoulders and make enemies of friends."

Muslim:C9B1N29 "Command For Fighting Against People So Long As They Do Not Profess That There Is No Ilah (God) But Allah And Muhammad Is His Messenger: When the Messenger breathed his last and Bakr was appointed Caliph, many Arabs chose to become apostates [rejected Islam]. Abu Bakr said: 'I will definitely fight against anyone who stops paying the Zakat tax, for it is an obligation. I will fight against them even to secure the cord used for hobbling the feet of a camel which they used to pay if they withhold it now.' Allah had justified fighting against those who refused to pay Zakat."

Muslim:C9B1N33 "The Prophet said: 'I have been commanded to fight against people till they testify there is no god but Allah, that Muhammad is the Messenger of Allah, and they establish prostration prayer, and pay Zakat. If they do it, their blood and property are protected.'"

Muslim:C10B1N176 "Muhammad (may peace be upon him) sent us in a raiding party. We raided Huraqat in the morning. I caught hold of a man and he said: 'There is no god but Allah,' but I attacked him with a spear anyway. It once occurred to me that I should ask the Apostle about this. The Messenger said: 'Did he profess "There is no god but Allah," and even then you killed him?' I said: 'He made a profession out of the fear of the weapon I was threatening him with.' The Prophet said: 'Did you tear out his heart in order to find out whether it had professed truly or not?'"

Muslim:C20B1N4597 "The Prophet said at the conquest of Mecca: 'There is no migration now, but only Jihad, fighting for the Cause of Islam. When you are asked to set out on a Jihad expedition, you should readily do so.'"

Muslim:C28B20N4628 "Allah has undertaken to provide for one who leaves his home to fight for His Cause and to affirm the truth of His word; Allah will either admit him to Paradise or will bring him back home with his reward and booty."

Muslim:C28B20N4629 "The Messenger said: 'One who is wounded in the Way of Allah - and Allah knows best who is wounded in His Way - will appear on the Day of Judgment with his wound still bleeding. The color (of its discharge) will be blood, (but) its smell will be musk.'"

Muslim:C34B20N4652-3 "The Merit Of Jihad And Of Keeping Vigilance Over The Enemy: A man came to the Holy Prophet and said: 'Who is the best of men?' He replied: 'A man who fights staking his life and spending his wealth in Allah's Cause.'"

Muslim:C42B20N4684 "A desert Arab came to the Prophet and said: 'Messenger, one man fights for the spoils of war; another fights that he may be remembered, and one fights that he may see his (high) position (achieved as a result of his valor in fighting). Which of these is fighting in the Cause of Allah?' The Messenger of Allah said: 'Who fights so that the word of Allah is exalted is fighting in the Way of Allah.'"

Muslim:C53B20N4717 "The Prophet said: 'This religion will continue to exist, and a group of people from the Muslims will continue to fight for its protection until the Hour is established.'"

Bukhari:V5B59N288 "I witnessed a scene that was dearer to me than anything I had ever seen. Aswad came to the Prophet while Muhammad was urging the Muslims to fight the pagans. He said, 'We shall fight on your right and on your left and in front of you and behind you.' I saw the face of the Prophet getting bright with happiness, for that saying delighted him."

Bukhari:V5B59N290 "The believers who did not join the Ghazwa [Islamic raid or invasion] and those who fought are not equal in reward."

Qur'an:2:193 "Fight them until there is no more Fitnah (disbelief) and religion is only for Allah. But if they cease/desist, let there be no hostility except against infidel disbelievers."

Qur'an:2:217 "They question you concerning fighting in the sacred month. Say: 'Fighting therein is a grave (matter); but to prevent access to Allah, to deny Him, to prevent access to the Sacred Mosque, to expel its members, and polytheism are worse than slaughter. Nor will they cease fighting you until they make you renegades from your religion. If any of you turn back and die in unbelief, your works will be lost and you will go to Hell. Surely those who believe and leave their homes to fight in Allah's Cause have the hope of Allah's mercy."

Qur'an:2:244 "Fight in Allah's Cause, and know that Allah hears and knows all."

Qur'an:2:246 "He said: 'Would you refrain from fighting if fighting were prescribed for you?' They said: 'How could we refuse to fight in Allah's Cause?'"

Ishaq:280 "The Apostle prepared for war in pursuance of Allah's command to fight his enemies and to fight the infidels who Allah commanded him to fight."

Qur'an:61:2 "O Muslims, why say one thing and do another? Grievously odious and hateful is it in the sight of Allah that you say that which you do not. Truly Allah loves those who fight in His Cause in a battle array, as if they were a solid cemented structure."

Bukhari:V4B52N61 "Allah's Apostle! We were absent from the first battle you fought against the pagans. If Allah gives us a chance to do battle, no doubt, He will see how bravely we fight."

Ishaq:398 "Ask them for their help. Thereby make the religion of Islam agreeable to them. And when you are resolved in the matter of religion concerning fighting your enemy you will have the advantage."

Qur'an:3:146 "How many prophets fought in Allah's Cause? With them (fought) myriads of godly men who were slain. They never lost heart if they met with disaster in Allah's Cause, nor did they weaken nor give in. Allah loves those who are firm and steadfast [warriors]."

Ishaq:393 "How many prophets has death in battle befallen and how many multitudes with him? They did not show weakness toward their enemies and were not humiliated when they suffered in the fight for Allah and their religion. That is steadfastness. Allah loves the steadfast."

Qur'an:3:153 "Behold! You ran off precipitately, climbing up the high hill without even casting a side glance at anyone, while the Messenger in your rear is calling you from your rear, urging you to fight. Allah gave you one distress after another by way of requital, to teach you not to grieve for the booty that had escaped you and for (the ill) that had befallen you."

Qur'an:3:154 "Say: 'Even if you had remained in your houses, those ordained to be slaughtered would have gone forth to the places where they were to slain."

Ishaq:440 "Helped by the Holy Spirit we smited Muhammad's foes. The Apostle sent a message to them with a sharp cutting sword."

Ishaq:470 "We attacked them fully armed, swords in hand, cutting through heads and skulls."

Qur'an:61:11 "Believers, shall I lead you to a bargain or trade that will save you from a painful torment? That you believe in Allah and His Messenger (Muhammad), and that you strive and fight in Allah's Cause with your property and your lives: That will be best for you!" Qur'an 61:12 "He will forgive you your sins, and admit you to Gardens under which rivers flow, and to beautiful mansions in Eden: that is indeed the Supreme Achievement. And another (favor) which you love: help from Allah for a speedy victory over your enemies."

Qur'an:8:5 "Your Lord ordered you out of your homes to fight for the true cause, even though some Muslims disliked it, and were averse (to fighting)."

Qur'an:24:53 "They swear their strongest oaths saying that if only you would command them. They would leave their homes (and go forth fighting in Allah's Cause). Say: 'Swear not; Obedience is (more) reasonable.'"

Qur'an:4:74 "Let those who fight in Allah's Cause sell this world's life for the hereafter. To him who fights in Allah's Cause, whether he is slain or victorious, We shall give him a reward."

Qur'an:4:75 "What reason have you that you should not fight in Allah's Cause?" [Another translation says:] "What is wrong with you that you do not fight for Allah?"

Qur'an:4:76 "Those who believe fight in the Cause of Allah."

Qur'an:4:77 "Have you not seen those to whom it was said: Withhold from fighting, perform the prayer and pay the zakat. But when orders for fighting were issued, a party of them feared men as they ought to have feared Allah. They say: 'Our Lord, why have You ordained fighting for us, why have You made war compulsory?'"

Qur'an:4:78 "Wherever you are, death will find you, even if you are in towers strong and high! So what is wrong with these people, that they fail to understand these simple words?"

Qur'an:4:84 "Then fight (Muhammad) in Allah's Cause. Incite the believers to fight with you."

Qur'an:4:94 "Believers, when you go abroad to fight wars in Allah's Cause, investigate carefully, and say not to anyone who greets you: 'You are not a believer!' Coveting the chance profits of this life (so that you may despoil him). With Allah are plenteous spoils and booty."

Qur'an:4:95 "Not equal are believers who sit home and receive no hurt and those who fight in Allah's Cause with their wealth and lives. Allah has granted a grade higher to those who fight with their possessions and bodies to those who sit home. Those who fight He has distinguished with a special reward."

Qur'an:4:100 "He who leaves his home in Allah's Cause finds abundant resources and many a refuge. Should he die as a refugee for Allah and His

Messenger His reward becomes due and sure with Allah. When you travel through the earth there is no blame on you if you curtail your worship for fear unbelievers may attack you. In truth the disbelievers are your enemy."

Qur'an:4:102 "When you (Prophet) lead them in prayer, let some stand with you, taking their arms with them. When they finish their prostrations, let them take positions in the rear. And let others who have not yet prayed come - taking all precaution, and bearing arms. The Infidels wish, if you were negligent of your arms, to assault you in a rush. But there is no blame on you if you put away your arms because of the inconvenience of rain or because you are ill; but take precaution. For the Unbelieving Infidels Allah hath prepared a humiliating punishment."

Qur'an:4:104 "And do not relent in pursuing the enemy."

May 2012

Edward Cline

CULTURE

Hollywood's Jihad Against America

> "During World War II Hollywood churned out combat pictures and home-front melodramas with the speed and efficiency that characterized so much war-time production. Those movies reflected a consensus that it was also their purpose to promote. The best of them were more than simple propaganda, but they tended to share a sense of clarity and purpose in their narrative structure as well as in their themes."

So wrote A.O. Scott in a *New York Times* Arts and Leisure feature on October 28, "A War on Every Screen: New Films Pegged to Iraq and Other Flash Points Are Awash in Ambiguity." After presenting brief synopses of several recent and forthcoming movies about the Iraq war and terrorism – most of them, to judge by his descriptions, viciously anti-American in theme and content – Scott concludes that they are "ambiguous," and semi-wistfully contrasts them with films produced during World War II. By "ambiguous" one can only suppose that he means they do not overtly condemn the U.S.

In that sense, they lack the "clarity and purpose" with which most World War II-era produced films were imbued.

Scott does, however, answer some of his own questions, and in the process identifies why, to him, at least, the films are "ambiguous."

> "What is missing in nearly every case is a sense of catharsis or illumination. This is hardly the fault of the filmmakers. Disorientation, ambivalence, a lack of clarity – these are surely

113

part of the collective experience they are trying to examine. How can you bring an individual story to a satisfying conclusion when nobody has any idea what the end of the larger story will look like?"

Much the same could be said about President Bush's Iraq policy. It is disoriented in its aims, now that it is a certainty that "democracy" will not work in a country whose citizens will continue to vote the straight Islamic ticket. It is ambivalent, measured by a purely emotional criterion. And, the policy lacks clarity, because the "insurgency" will never end if its promoters and paymasters remain untouched by American military might. That is the "larger" story whose resolution no one can as yet predict.

Although Scott's article rambles on in search of answers, he does make an occasional true observation.

> "...[T]he public may well succeed in avoiding them [the films discussed by Scott]....Public indifference...may bolster the ideologically convenient notion that Hollywood is out of touch with the American people, and also the economically convenient idea that people go to the movies to escape the problems of the world rather than to confront them."

I do not think the idea that Hollywood is out of touch with the American people needs bolstering or that it is "convenient," unless the term is Scott's substitute for "logical." Ever since the mid-1960's Hollywood has waged a campaign of hate of the U.S. and has left few left-wing or collectivist issues untouched or un-dramatized. Nor is the idea that people go to the movies to be inspired or at least "entertained" an illogical one, either. Both ideas are true.

> "What is notable about this new crop of war movies is not their earnestness or their didacticism – traits many of them undoubtedly display – but rather their determination to embrace confusion, complexity, and ambiguity."

The new crop of movies are that way because it is their makers' intent to leave American movie-goers confused about the issues, baffled by their "complexity," and in doubt about any possible resolution. The ambiguity plays an insidious role. It injects doubt into the issues and into the minds of American viewers. That is their earnest, Existentialist, "didactic" method. The ambiguity is not an accident or a consequence of confusion or an attempt to avoid what Scott calls "finger-wagging" and "sloganeering." The ambiguity is deliberate, and it is indeed the "fault" of the filmmakers.

Although much of Hollywood during World War II was under the thumb of leftists, they did not dare insult the intelligence of the American public or attack their values or patriotism by offering films that were ambiguous about the nature of the enemy or the enormity of the effort required to defeat him. They did not begin to crawl out into the light until after the war.

Today, the enemy, Islamism or Islamofascism, is not identified as an enemy, and if Islamists are hostile to the U.S., according to Hollywood, it is the fault of the U.S. To Hollywood, the Islamists can slaughter thousands, regardless of their religion or politics, and they remain innocent. They were "conditioned" by circumstances and cannot be blamed for their actions, no matter how horrendous or murderous. Only the U.S. is blameworthy, because it is a giant.

If a handful of American soldiers run amok and commit "crimes" against members of what is (in fact) an enemy population, that deserves feature length attention. If innumerable *jihadists* plot to detonate bombs in New York and Boston, Hollywood will not deign to dramatize it, but ask, instead: Who can blame them?

Every one of the movies Scott discusses is a multi-million dollar instance of agitprop whose purpose is not to instill or uphold moral values, but to subvert and destroy them by instilling guilt in Americans, to make them doubt the value of being Americans. If a modern war movie is not weepy, whiny, or "grieving," then it is blatantly nihilistic.

Parenthetically, it is a measure of America's cultural malaise that weeping, grieving and maudlin commiseration have become the especial foci of news reportage, regardless of the tragedy or catastrophe. "Grief" and "suffering" rank just behind "sacrifice" and "selflessness" as touchstones of moral worth. I date the beginning of this sordid element of national self-pitying back to October 1983, when terrorists killed over two hundred Marines and other U.S. servicemen in their Beirut barracks, an assault that President Ronald Reagan failed to answer. As the stream of flag-draped coffins arrived in the U.S., the news media embarked on an orgy of "grief" and "doubt." Did any one call for retaliation against the responsible terrorist groups or the state that sponsored them and demand that Reagan take action? I don't recall.

Scott comes close to grasping the connection between the movies whose "ambiguous" purposes he ponders and the nature of the Iraq and Afghanistan conflicts.

> "We have been told from the start, by both the administration and its critics, that this will be a long, complicated, episodic fight. And so attempts to make sense of it piecemeal and in medias res, in discrete narratives with beginnings and ends, are likely to feel incomplete and unsatisfying."

He comes close, and might have understood the nature of the conflicts, were he not also a pawn of the filmmakers' purposes, which is to inculcate doubt, confusion, and disgust. Were he able to delve into more fundamental issues, he might have asked the questions:

Are we there to ensure that no Islamic state ever attacks America again? And if we are, what is the best means of accomplishing that end? Or are we there motivated by some Wilsonian notion of spreading "democracy" as a moral duty, to indulge in what Progressive writer Herbert Croly called the "tonic of a moral adventure"? Is there a vital connection between Bush's Christian policy of warfighting and why the U.S. will continue to expend blood and treasure in a futile campaign to win the "hearts and minds" of a people who prefer to adhere to a Dark Age morality? Is a code of self-sacrifice one of life or of death?

Finally, he might have asked: If Hollywood had turned out these kinds of movies during World War II, might not the filmmakers have been boycotted by the public, or charged with treason, or, at the very least, tarred and feathered and run out of town?

I do not plan to see any of the movies discussed by A.O. Scott in his article. I know what they are about just by watching the morning newscasts for free. My kinds of war movies are the 1939 *Four Feathers*, and *Glory, Hamburger Hill, Gunga Din, Hell is for Heroes*, and many others that, among other things, not the least of which is their cleaner, unambiguous esthetics, inspire me to fight my own battles.

October 2007

116

Kipling's Remonstrance: "An Imperial Rescript"

Rudyard Kipling's verse is little known today. The wisdom one can find in it would not fit into the modern pedagogical philosophy of unreason, political correctness, and conformity. After all, he was an unapologetic champion of the West, of the second British Empire, in particular, an unabashed but not uncritical "cultural imperialist." Most students -- indeed, most writers and thinkers today -- are ignorant of Kipling, if not hostile to him. He died in January 1936, when the world he had known had changed for the worse, and was marching toward war and collectivism and horrors unimaginable to him in the 19th century.

But, as early as 1890, at the age of 25, in "An Imperial Rescript,"* he took a marvelously adept poetic swipe at consensual collectivism, which, before he could imagine it ever happening in his lifetime, would impoverish his own country and many more nations in the next century. The opus begins:

> Now this is the tale of the Council the German Kaiser decreed,
> To ease the strong of their burden, to help the weak in their need.
> He sent word to the peoples, who struggle, and pant, and sweat,
> That the straw might be counted fairly and the tally of bricks be set.

In short, representatives of all the productive men from around the globe -- the "Lords of Their Hands" -- were summoned to wait upon the Kaiser's Council and hear a master plan for eliminating exploitation, injustice, unregulated commerce and labor, and other alleged social ills throughout the world. It is implied in the second stanza that men were crying out against those ills, and that the Kaiser heard their complaints.

The third stanza goes:

And the young King said -- "I have found it, the road to the rest ye seek:
"The strong shall wait for the weary, the hale shall halt for the weak:
"With the even tramp of an army where no man breaks from the line,
"Ye shall march to peace and plenty in the bond of brotherhood -- sign!"

But, the productive men pause before they sign the document that would fetter each man to the next. Just as they are about to indenture themselves to mutual servitude, someone laughs. Not Howard Roark. Not John Galt.

In 1890, it was too early for that particular literary "No!" to be flung out at the world.

> A hand was stretched to the goose-quill, a fist was cramped to scrawl,
> When -- the laugh of a blue-eyed maiden ran clear through the Council-hall.

What did this maiden represent? Was she laughing at the foolishness of what the men were submitting to? Why did the productive men pause?

And the Spirit of Man that is in Him to the light of the vision woke;
And the men drew back from the paper, as the Yankee delegate spoke: --

Each man has second thoughts about what he is about to agree to. Kipling allows an American the first objection:

> "There's a girl in Jersey City who works on the telephone;
> "We're going to hitch our horses and dig for a house of our own,
> "With gas and water connections, and steam heat through to the top;
> "And. W. Hohenzollern, I guess I shall work till I drop."

Then a Briton proudly reiterates the ownership of one's life and purpose:

And an English delegate thundered: -- "The weak an' the lame be blowed!
"I've a berth in the Sou'-West workshops, a home in the Wandsworth Road;
"And till the 'sociation has footed my buryin' bill,
"I work for the kids an' the missus. Pull up! I'll be damned if I will!"

By the ninth stanza, the Kaiser's Council goes into consultation about what to do about this revolt of the men they only want to help by relieving them of the "burden" of freedom. Here Kipling permits himself a kind of humor possible only to a man who takes ideas seriously. The Council passes a resolution:

> "But till we are built like angels -- with hammer and chisel and pen,
> "We will work for ourselves and a woman, for ever and ever, amen."

Modern "free verse" is replete with random concretes connected to no abstractions, not even esthetic ones. Kipling's poem here contains many concretes that express a pair of metaphysical and political abstractions: individualism and collectivism.

Kipling was on to something: A glimmer of mutual slavery, of true democracy, of chain gangs, and unions -- of the nature and consequences of collectivism. And he offered an antidote to it: a reminder to men of the purpose of life. The laughing maiden represents, as far as one can tell, the joy of life. The benevolent rays of the early sunset of reason in his time permitted him to champion independence and individualism. His productive men remember why they work and live, and refuse to become slaves or to enslave each other.

What an overture! What wisdom! And what a literary ancestor of Ayn Rand was Rudyard Kipling! She was our own laughing maiden, who reminded us all!

Notes:
1. Rescript -- a sovereign's or government edict or announcement.
2. Hohenzollern -- a German dynasty that ruled from 1192 to 1918.
3. 'sociation -- An association, or voluntary, private mutual aid or welfare organization, to which workers paid a small subscription, and which acted much like an insurance company.

Rudyard Kipling: The Complete Verse. 1890. London: Kyle Cathie Ltd. (1990). pp. 230-231

February 2006

The Ignoble Nobel Peace Prize

One searches in vain through the whole list of Nobel Peace Prize winners from 1901 to the present for a single laureate whose work measurably advanced the cause of peace. The term *peace* itself, as it is employed by the Nobel Committee, on the surface is wishful and ethereal. The Peace Prize has, as a rule, recognized peace efforts which have unfailingly come to naught. Why? The "peace" pined for is essentially a Kantian concept. It is disconnected from reality. Work for peace, urges the Committee, even if your efforts are spoiled by war and conflict. Peace is good for its own sake. Work for peace as though you wished it to become a maxim, a moral rule.

The "peace" sought after and rewarded by the Nobel Committee is an unconditional peace that admits no legitimate grounds for war or conflict - - nor any rational grounds for peace or war. Alfred Nobel set the original terms for the Peace Prize in 1895 when he said that it should be given to "the person who shall have done the most or the best work for fraternity between nations, for the abolition or reduction of standing armies and for the holding and promotion of peace congresses." In 1895, Nobel might have had a different idea of a "fraternity between nations," which certainly could not have included the conquest or subjugation of one nation by another. Still, it is an altruistic statement of pacifism.

The Nobel Peace Prize discards the concept of the initiation of force by one country against another -- or by one individual against another -- as a criterion for evaluation, and substitutes an inverted moral judgment. The wishes of the initiator of force should be treated just as legitimate as the wishes of his victim. If the victim resists, war or conflict result. That is bad. Violence ensues. Ergo, the victim must compromise and cede some or all of the initiator's wishes, if there is to be any "peace."

Thus, for example, the continuing pressure on Israel to sacrifice its existence to the likes of Yassir Arafat, Hamas and other killers and predators. Or the pressure on the U.S. to not defend itself against its attackers, or to sign the Kyoto Treaty that would destroy what is left of its industrial base.

It is a premise shared by the Nobel Committee, and by most of the laureates, benign, disreputable, and indifferent alike. Thus the Prize's futility. It is, appropriately, a Kantian trophy of no consequence, a blue ribbon for good intentions. Thorbjoern Jagland, former Norwegian prime minister who chaired the five-member selection committee (elected to the committee by the Norwegian parliament), defended the committee's choice against charges that Obama had accomplished nothing to deserve the award.

> "We are not awarding the prize for what may happen in the future but for what [Obama] has done in the previous year…We would hope this will enhance what he is trying to do."

Jagland also explained away the fact that Obama was nominated for the prize about two weeks into his presidency, before he had a chance to move on any item on his agenda.

> "Some people say — and I understand it — 'Isn't it premature? Too early?' Well, I'd say then that it could be too late to respond three years from now," Thorbjoern Jagland, chairman of the Norwegian Nobel Committee, told the AP. "It is now that we have the opportunity to respond — all of us."

> Jagland said the committee whittled down a record pool of 205 nominations and had "several candidates until the last minute," but it became more obvious that "we couldn't get around these deep changes that are taking place" under Obama.

Those promised "deep changes" -- meaning, among other things, the virtual regimentation of the American economy -- are what moved Jagland and his colleagues to nominate Obama based solely on his campaign rhetoric, before Obama had a chance to routinely retreat to the Rose Garden to enjoy a Marlboro. In short, they awarded him the Peace Prize before he had won the election. That's the Chicago way: pretend for legal reasons to solicit open bids for a government contract, while having already chosen who's going to get it.

A gold medallion and a sack of cash will recognize the unrealized "efforts" of an American president, Barack Obama, who, to date, has failed to keep any of his socialist promises to transform America into a European collectivist knock-off -- though he has helped to lay the foundation of totalitarianism here. In tune with Obama's continuing campaign slogan, the Nobel committee awarded Obama the prize in the "hope" that he will indeed "change" the U.S. into something with which it and its fellow anti-American European manqués would be more comfortable: a whipped giant, chained to servitude and sacrifice for the sake of the global poor, the environment, "social justice," and other "global challenges."

The reaction to the announcement of Obama's Nobel Peace Prize win has been, to say the least, "polarized." Daniel Pipes notes that "the absurdity of the prize decision will hurt Obama politically in the United States, contrasting his role as international celebrity with his record devoid of accomplishments." The Taliban and other Islamic gangs and spokesmen also made the same observation, demanding, "Show us the money!"

Media Matters, the left-wing mouthpiece of liberals and Democrats, responded immediately to any and all criticism of Obama's win in a posting, "Still rooting against America: Right-wing media use Nobel Prize announcement as excuse to attack Obama," and included links to several "right-wingers'" statements about the Nobel decision. That no one should need an "excuse" to attack Obama is beyond the grasp of these collectivists. He has provided Americans with numerous *reasons*, not including his three dozen or so "czars."

Bloomberg News also provided links to reactions to the announcement, some of the statements indiscriminately witless with delight, others dour and disappointed. "It sets the seal on America's return to the heart of all the world's peoples," French President Nicholas Sarkozy wrote to Obama. Those questioning whether he deserved the prize included Fawzi Barhoum, a Hamas spokesman in the Gaza Strip. "There's a lot more that Obama needs to achieve for peace and for the Palestinian people in order to receive this award," Barhoum said in a telephone interview.

Iran also sputtered raspberries.

> Ali Akbar Javanfekr, media aide to Iranian President Mahmoud Ahmadinejad told AFP: "We hope that this gives (Obama) the incentive to walk in the path of bringing justice to the world order...We are not upset and we hope that by receiving this prize he will start taking practical steps to remove injustice in the world."

This is Javanfekr raising his voice to be heard over this noisy tug-of-war between Pecksniffian mental astaticism and Islamic nose-wrinkling Obama, ever ready to comment on anything, expressed surprise at winning the Peace Prize. Obama also wished to be heard above the din of applause:

> To be honest, I do not feel that I deserve to be in the company of so many of the transformative figures who've been honored by this prize -- men and women who've inspired me and inspired the entire world through their courageous pursuit of peace.

Translation: Why didn't Saul Alinsky win the Peace Prize? He transformed me! Besides, I really don't know who else has won it, except maybe Al Gore, and that Southern cracker, Jimmy Carter. I looked up the list of past winners, and can't even pronounce half their names.

True to the Nobel Committee's "party line" and explanations of why it awarded the Prize to a non-achiever, Obama noted:

> That is why I've said that I will accept this award as a call to action, a call for all nations and all peoples to confront the common challenges of the 21st century. These challenges won't all be met during my presidency, or even my lifetime. But I know these challenges can be met so long as it's recognized that they will not be met by one person or one nation alone.

This is true. All those "challenges" require the employment of force to effect the changes to bring the U.S. more into line with a collectivized and increasingly barbaric world.

> This award -- and the call to action that comes with it -- does not belong simply to me or my administration; it belongs to all people around the world who have fought for justice and for peace. And most of all, it belongs to you, the men and women of America, who have dared to hope and have worked so hard to make our world a little better.

Such *faux* humility sounds more like an Oscar speech than an acknowledgement; one keeps imagining him clutching a statuette, with his eyes glazing over to keep back the tears.

But, no, thank you, Mr. President. You keep it. By the terms of the Nobel Committee, you earned it. To your everlasting ignominy.

October 2009

The "Sensitivity" Syndrome

There is no retreat but in submission and slavery! Our chains are forged!...It is vain, sir, to extenuate the matter. Gentlemen may cry peace, peace – but there is no peace. The war is actually begun! The next gale that sweeps from the north will bring to our ears the clash of resounding arms! – Patrick Henry, March 23, 1775

Yes, the war declared by the Islamists on the West began years ago – nay, decades ago – but gentlemen raised on Western pragmatism and multiculturalism continue to cry peace, peace, even though the clash has caused tens of thousands of deaths and incalculable destruction – but no echo of resounding arms. The enemy will be content only with the peace of our submission and slavery, and are exploiting the multiculturalism that has forged the chains being fitted onto men's minds.

The second definition of *syndrome*, in *The American Heritage Dictionary*, is that it is "a group of signs and symptoms that collectively indicate or characterize a disease, psychological disorder, or other abnormal condition." The three ingredients of what could be called the "sensitivity" syndrome include pragmatism, multiculturalism and *fear*. It is a syndrome not conducive to conducting business or exercising one's freedom of speech, if one refrains from taking certain actions for fear of hurting the feelings of unknown persons who may or may not retaliate with violence. In this instance, the syndrome is indicative of de facto censorship.

The Random House decision in May to cancel the publication of Sherry Jones' novel, *The Jewel of Medina*, about Mohammad's child bride, Aisha, represents two developments fatal to the First Amendment and the future of freedom of speech: it is a capitulation to the "cautionary advice" that the novel might be considered "offensive" to Muslims and possibly spark a wave of violent "protest" similar to that which followed the publication of the Danish Mohammad cartoons in 2005; and it is an implicit injunction against other publishers banning the publication of any literary work that depicts Mohammad.

The Belfast Telegraph ("Next 'Satanic Verses' is shelved for fear of stirring up Islamic extremists") and other newspapers reported on August 9 (from a Reuters report of August 7) that:

"Random House deputy publisher Thomas Perry said in a statement the company received 'cautionary advice not only that the publication of his book might be offensive to some in the Muslim community, but also that it could incite acts of violence by a small, radical segment.'"

Like the other newspapers, the Telegraph did not fully quote Perry. The complete statement, carried in The Wall Street Journal article of August 6, "You Still Can't Write About Muhammad," reads that Random House received the "cautionary advice" from "credible and unrelated sources."

"We decided," went the Random House press release, "after much deliberation, to postpone publication for the safety of the author, employees of Random House, booksellers and anyone else who would be involved in distribution and sale of the novel."

The sources are certainly "credible" but hardly "unrelated," as will be discussed below. And the "small, radical segment" of Muslims is nothing less than a large band of killers, extortionists and fifth columnists funded by organizations with financial links to Saudi Arabia, Iran and other Islamic regimes.

The irony of Random House's decision is that the novel apparently does not paint Mohammad in critical terms. "I have deliberately and consciously written respectfully about Islam and Mohammad," said Jones. "I envisioned that my book would be a bridge-builder."

A "bridge-builder"? To connect what? The Western value of individualism and a separation of church and state, and the Eastern value of mysticism and the union of religion and state? Kipling was right. Fundamentally, the twain between East and West can never meet – unless one capitulates to the other by abandoning or surrendering its values.

The Belfast Telegraph wrote that:

"The novel traces the life of Aisha from her engagement to Mohammad, when she was six, until the Prophet's death."

Jones said, "They did have a great love story. [!!!] He died with his head on her breast."

The Telegraph said that Jones, "who has never visited the Middle East, spent several years studying Arab history. The novel, she says, is a synthesis of all she had learnt." Which was, in essence, absolutely nothing about Islam and how it is, by its nature, virulently obsessed with global conquest. Jones apparently had no objection to a barbarian raping a six – or nine-year-old girl, and the "love story" she novelized was woven from whole cloth.

The Wall Street Journal opinion piece, written by Muslim Asra Q. Nomani, even contains an excerpt from Aisha's wedding night: "The pain of consummation soon melted away. Muhammad was so gentle. I hardly felt the scorpion's sting. To be in his arms, skin to skin, was the bliss I had longed for all my life."

All *nine years*? That kind of writing should have appeared in a Harlequin Romance style bodice-ripper that celebrated pedophilia and child molestation. But, under the imprint of a major publisher, Ballantine, a subsidiary of Random House?

But Jones' ignorance of and naiveté about Islam and the publisher's tastelessness are irrelevant. Random House ought to have been free to publish her novel without fear of consequence, except for the probable loss of its investment in the book. (Jones received a $100,000 advance for that title and a sequel.) More likely than making waves as a literary work, it would have been lost in the swamp of undifferentiated fiction that publishers gurgitate every year. Muslims who might have objected to it – their "sensitivities" or feelings having been abused – might not have even become aware of its existence.

The New York Times, once a champion of freedom of speech but now a yeah-sayer in political correctness and "sensitivity," merely noted the development in a one-paragraph article on August 9, "Random House Cancels Novel with Islamic Themes."

> "Carol Schneider, a spokeswoman for Random House, said on Friday that the company 'requested that it be postponed indefinitely' after consulting with experts and receiving unsolicited advice. 'We thought it was not a good time, with tensions running as high as they do, to publish this,' Ms. Schneider said."

No, Muslims might have remained oblivious to the novel's existence, but for Denise A. Spellberg, associate professor of history and Middle Eastern Studies at the University of Texas at Austin. According to most of the newspaper and wire service reports, it was she who unleashed the dogs of fear.

Having been sent an advance copy of *The Jewel of Medina* by Random House, in hopes of her writing a jacket blurb endorsing the novel, Spellberg's first action after reading it was to call a Muslim and guest lecturer in Spellberg's classes, Shahed Amanullah, to warn him about the book because, she said, according to the WSJ article, the novel "made fun of Muslims and their history" and that she found the novel "incredibly offensive." Amanullah subsequently emailed other Muslims about the book, even though he had not read it and was taking her word for it.

The next day Spellberg called Random House/Knopf editor Jane Garrett with dire warnings about the consequences of publishing the book, calling its scheduled publication a "declaration of war," a "national security issue," and claiming that the novel was "far more controversial than [Salman Rushdie's] *The Satanic Verses* and the Danish cartoons." How anyone could imagine that Jones' novel could have been any of those things is only a clue to the inflated importance Spellberg must place on her role in "building bridges," multiculturalist "bridges" which she would not want to see burned in defense of someone else's freedom of speech. (And this is one example of how multiculturalism is anti-Western and a destroyer.)

It is not so curious that, having first alerted the Muslim grapevine about the book – surely with the knowledge that some "extremist" or "radicalized" Muslims just might want to conspire to bomb Random House's offices or set up picket lines outside of them or murder Jones in "protest" of the novel – Spellberg then warned the publisher of those very dangers. This is tantamount to setting a fire in a crowded theater, then shouting "Fire!" Draw your own conclusions about her motivation, but whatever the conclusion, her actions were contemptible.

Random House's executives and editors, "sensitive" to these dangers, some two weeks later terminated Jones' publishing contract, freeing her to shop the novel with other publishers. This "sensitivity" was not a reflection of their "respect" for Islam and Muslims, but of their fear of violence and even possible lawsuits.

In a letter to the WSJ on August 9, "I Didn't Kill 'The Jewel of Medina,'" Spellberg accuses Nomani of "falsely" asserting that she was the "instigator" behind Random House's decision, blithely forgetting that but for her actions, no one would have paid any serious attention to Jones' novel.

In her letter, Spellberg asserts that as an "expert on Aisha's life, I felt it was my professional responsibility to counter this novel's fallacious representation of a very real woman's life." How could she be an "expert" on the life of a figure who may or may not have existed? Islam's "history" is no more credible or factually based than is Christianity's, completely absent of proof, relying mostly on tongue-in-cheek episodes invented by theologians and scribes for the sake of the gullible and the credulous. Spellberg is as much an "authority" on Aisha as Sherry Jones.

Spellberg further claims in her letter that she does not "espouse censorship of any kind, but I do value my right to critique those who abuse the past without regard for its richness or resonance in the present." But the kind of censorship she instigated was a cabal whose specific purpose was to stop the publication of a book with which she disagreed. Instead, she lays blame for the decision – one with which she agrees – entirely on the doorstep of Random House.

One is at a loss to fault Random House for caving in to the hypothetical dangers of publishing Jones' novel. Weighing the possible expenses of fortifying its business offices against Muslim terrorists and protecting the lives of anyone connected with Jones' novel – certainly an *abnormal* condition of existence – one can hardly blame the publisher for its decision. What is regarded as "normal" today is a perceived necessity to defer to the threat of harassment or physical force.

After all, Random House has been paying taxes to our government to protect it from domestic criminals and foreign invaders – to ensure its enjoyment of the First Amendment without risk of molestation by any party, religious, "offended" or otherwise – a task which, vis-à-vis Islamists, our government has not performed with a shred of effectiveness.

Where would we be today if men were "sensitive" to the tensions that led to Lexington and Concord and Bunker Hill, and decided it "was not a good time" to take a stand? There were men like that in 18th century America, but fortunately their "cautionary advice" was ignored. The "sensitivity" syndrome has made modern Americans *insensible* to what they have been surrendering and giving up.

The gales have been sweeping from the north for over a generation, but today's gentlemen either ignore them or do not notice them.

128

August 2008

The "Sensitivity" Syndrome: II

One wishes that courage was spent on causes and actions worthy of the virtue. Last August, in "The 'Sensitivity' Syndrome," I commented on Random House's cancellation of the publication of Sherry Jones's *The Jewel of Medina*, a kind of feminist "bodice-ripper" novel about Aisha, the child-bride of Mohammad, for fear of Islamic "extremist" violence. The novel, if published in August as planned by Ballantine, a subsidiary of Random House, I noted, would have quickly sunk out of sight into the morass of mediocre fiction which the trade regularly churns out, but for the efforts of a non-Muslim provocateur, associate professor of history and Middle Eastern Studies at the University of Texas at Austin, Denise Spellberg.

Spellberg was sent a review copy by the publisher for her endorsement in the form of a jacket blurb. Instead, she first warned the Muslim grapevine that it offended Islam, and the next day warned Random House of possible "extremist violence." She claimed, among other things, that the "sacred history" of Mohammad had been turned by Jones into "soft core pornography."

> "I do have a problem with the deliberate misinterpretation of history," she claimed in an email. What she apparently does not have a problem with is inciting violence among Muslims, who, without Spellberg's calling attention to the novel, might have remained ignorant of its existence. What any other writer should have a problem with was her calculated conspiracy to see the novel unpublished through censorship by fear. She called the novel a "very ugly, stupid piece of work." That description more aptly applies to Spellberg's actions.

The publication rights to the novel were bought by a small British publisher, Gibson Square, which has published other controversial books, including Londonistan, by Melanie Phillips, which details the gradual submission of Britain and the British government to Islam, and Blow up Russia, by Alexander Litvinenko, who was murdered by Vladimir Putin's agents in London.

.

On September 27, Muslims firebombed the London home of Martin Rynja, the Dutch publisher and owner of Gibson Square. Rynja's home also served as the offices of the book-publishing firm. Gibson Square announced on September 5 that it had bought the publication rights to

Jones's novel and planned to publish it. Another small publisher, Beaufort Books of New York, in cooperation with Gibson Square, plans to publish *The Jewel of Medina* in the U.S., and has signed a contract for its sequel. Last Monday Beaufort Books closed its office as a precaution against similar censorship by violence. Rynja is presumably now in hiding or under police protection, and publication of the novel in Britain or in the U.S. remains to be seen.

Three Muslims have been arrested, two of them outside Rynja's home. That aspect of the incident is curious. Scotland Yard's Special Branch, in an undisclosed undercover operation, had knowledge of the conspiracy to firebomb the house and presumably murder Rynja, who was told to leave. The police waited for two of the suspects to actually commit the arson by shoving a container of gas through Rynja's letterbox, which ignited inside the house, before collaring the two Muslims. Then the police and firefighters had to break down the front door to extinguish the fire. The house is now vacant.

So one might wonder why the police waited until the Muslims had actually committed a crime they were certain was going to occur, instead of arresting them before Rynja was compelled to leave and his home was damaged. The police's odd behavior is linked to the fear of the authorities of being accused of racial or religious "profiling," an illogical policy that debilitates Britain's counter-terrorism efforts (and also the U.S.'s).

Aside from the presumed undercover operation that netted them knowledge of the suspects' intentions, the police refused to risk arresting two Muslims who were walking around London with an incendiary device at two o'clock in the morning in the vicinity of the intended victim's neighborhood as not grounds enough for action. That is, the police and the courts would have likely accepted the Muslim position that it was not grounds enough for action. This is another face of the "sensitivity syndrome" that is requisite for submission to Islam and Sharia law.

Leaving aside Rynja's literary esteem for Jones's novel – "I was completely bowled over by the novel and the moving love story it portrays," he said weeks before the firebombing – Rynja expressed the proper moral position against censorship by firebombing, government edict, or by popular opinion. "I immediately felt that it was imperative to publish it. In an open society there has to be open access to literary works, regardless of fear."

131

Going by descriptions of *The Jewel of Medina*, I do not plan to read the novel.

> "Described by critics as a tale of 'lust, love and intrigue in the Prophet's harem,' *The Jewel of Medina* traces the life of Aisha, Mohammed's favorite wife. It tells of her marriage aged nine to Mohammed, who is much older, and how she is forced to use her wits and sword to defend her position as he takes another 12 wives and concubines," reported the Daily Mail.

> "The novel also tells how, at 14, Aisha almost betrays her husband after they are separated as they travel together. She is rescued by a childhood friend who tries to seduce her. She resists, but the scandal rocks Medina. When she returns, a mob accuses her of adultery. Mohammed's friends urge him to divorce her, but he tells them: 'I would just as soon cut out my own heart.'"

Not exactly on the level of Othello. But one imagines that Muslim objections to the novel dwell on the portrayals of Aisha as a Wahhabist Wonder Woman and of Mohammad as a guy with a heart of gold who wouldn't dream of allowing his favorite wife to be stoned to death or beheaded on the rumor that she had committed adultery, which is the kind of punishment that Saudi and other theocratic courts mete out to wayward women. Aisha's and Mohammad's actions contradict Islamic moral and social norms; those actions are at variance with Sharia law; therefore Muslims are offended by the novel and oppose its publication.

And oppose the novel they do, and any form of representation of Mohammad in word or picture, as the reaction to the Danish cartoons demonstrated in 2005, or any criticism of Islam or Muslims that could be interpreted as "religious hatred" or "incitement" to it by both Muslims and Britain's suborned judicial system. One Muslim cleric, Omar Bakri, was outspoken about the fate of those who were in any way associated with publication of *The Jewel of Medina*, that the firebombing of Rynja's home was but "the thin edge of the wedge."

Another Muslim cleric also weighed in.

> "…[T]he radical cleric Anjem Choudhary said the book was an insult to the Prophet Mohammed's honor, something he said would warrant a 'death penalty' under Sharia law."

Note the qualifier in Choudhary's description as a "radical" cleric. This is also a form of "sensitivity," which blanks out the fact that any Muslim cleric must be "radical" by definition of Sharia law and its imposition on both Muslims and non-Muslims. There is no "moderate," conciliatory form of Islam, just as there can be no such thing as a "moderate" Muslim willing to observe secular law at the price of compromising his religious beliefs. Islamic clerics warn of punishment of Muslims who do recognize the validity of secular law. An Islam that made such a concession to secular law would no longer be Islam, no longer be "extreme," and no longer be a threat to the West.

Compare the Telegraph article with that of the New York Times of September 29, "Attack May Be Tied to Book About Muhammad." It "may be"? Was Rynja being threatened by Christian Scientists or Jehovah's Witnesses, or by members of Holiness, a branch of the Mennonites? Submission to Islam is evident on both sides of the Atlantic.

Of course, a sample of official Islamic mental gymnastics may be seen in a Daily Telegraph opinion piece from 2004, "We need protection from the pedlars of religious hatred," by the secretary-general of the Muslim Council of Britain.

There is no point in warning that the same brand of submission to Islam can happen in the U.S. It already has, as the action of Random House has demonstrated, and also the evasive manner in which especially the federal government and the news media sensitively treat Islamic "extremism."

Sensitivity's other name is self-censorship, and opposition to it has been fallen to small publishers and those who would defend them at renewed risk, such as Salman Rushdie, subject of a similar fatwa of reprisals in 1989 for The Satanic Verses. The champions of the freedom of speech have always been in a minority, and very often they have made a difference. Never minding its literary value, we should hope that Sherry Jones's *The Jewel of Medina* sees the light of day.

October 2008

THE WIZARDS OF DISAMBIGUATION

A Critique of Mystery Genre Criticism

> Mystery writers generally have to work too hard applying what they know, to learn the techniques of expressing it in criticism. – Ross MacDonald, *Inward Journey*

The genesis of this essay is peculiar. I was invited by Western Michigan University Press to write an article for an anthology of articles about detective and crime fiction. I wrote the piece, called "The Wizards of Disambiguation," which burst the balloons of various left-wing literary critics who alleged that Dashiell Hammett's *The Maltese Falcon* was a kind of proletarian novel. In the piece I prove that, while Hammett had Red sympathies, his hero, Sam Spade, wasn't some kind of signifying avatar of communist ideology and that all the Frankfurt School-inspired "deconstructive" interpretations of the novel were just so much hooey. The piece wasn't accepted. It turned out, I learned later on, that all the other essays in that anthology were written by left-wing critics. But the exercise led me to write an answer to *The Maltese Falcon*, set in the same week and year as Hammett's story, which was originally serialized in Black Mask Magazine in 1928. Thus was born China Basin, set in 1928 San Francisco, finished in 1990.

I have always nurtured a sharp dislike and mistrust of the presumptuous of authorities who try to "do good" by resorting to force or penalties, and whose means to the end of coerced conformity has been either to control actions or things, or to eradicate them altogether, for one's own "good," for the public's, or both. This hostility was bred when, as a child, I was obliged to deal with patronizing county social workers. Since then, over a period of decades, I have witnessed the government insinuate its presence into virtually every area of American life.

The presumptuousness of expanding government power is based on a corroded notion of freedom among modern Americans, who are willing to tolerate the expansion, which notion fuels the ceaseless activism of those in and out of political office who wish to impose that presence on a populace that has yet to show any sign of revolt against the presumptuous ministrations of control and regulation. The presumption is closed to reason, and communicated to us unchecked, in large part, by our education system and the "news media," both of which treat the phenomenon and the morality of statism as unchallengeable givens in the pursuit of unassailable populist or social ideals.

To question the prerogatives of legislative or regulatory power is to invite gasps of shock or dumbfoundedness or even outrage. Reason, after all, assumes a value in truth, and truth today is either unwelcome in the parlors of many men's minds, or is unrecognizable, or has been demoted to a rank lower than that of a wish, or often is not even present in the hierarchy of "collective" values.

This presumptuousness is so endemic that it is hardly topical. When was the last time your child came home from school and said, "Our civics teacher said that the President's State of the Union speech was overtly Orwellian – the President equated 'freedom' with 'duty' and married a whole bunch of other antithetical concepts, and that we'd better watch out"? When was the last time your son or daughter wrote home from college to report that "Our economics professor demonstrated how all those federal studies on smoking, the ozone layer, nutrition, health costs, the environment, food preservatives – well, you name it – are based on statistics and pseudo-science, and produced by semi-private firms that'll produce any 'evidence' the government wants, just to keep getting federal grant money"?

When was the last time you heard a television newscaster express concern that the latest Supreme Court ruling or Act of Congress was a certifiable abridgement of speech, property, or the freedom of association, and turn to his fellow script-reader and say, "Carol here went to Thomas Jefferson University today and spoke with Professor Hughes, the out-spoken critic of Federalism, and got his thoughts on the implications of this move for all of us. Carol? ..."?

Chances are that unsubstantiated assertions regarding all political, economic, and "social" issues are passed on to your children as rock solid verities, and their grades made dependent on how well they parrot them. And more likely than not the television newscaster will deliver news of the latest sabotage of the Constitution or of the latest Congressional assault on the electorate with an air of smug, vacuous,

uncritical righteousness. In our culture, it is becoming more and more the rule that the dispensers of knowledge and news are the *least* trustworthy or credible sources of truth.

By the same token, there is much in modern literary criticism that I find utterly divorced from reason and truth. Modern criticism has as little to do with criticism as has phrenology or horoscopy. It is so far removed from reason and truth that it often takes on the dreaminess of an elaborate, dreary, belabored fantasy whose denouement rides on the interpretation of mystical runes. Much of it is so blatantly irrational and absurd that one is continually astonished that professors can teach it and columnists parrot it with a straight face.

Yet these same professors of literature and book reviewers and literary commentators and dispensers of knowledge and news have been teaching it and repeating it in earnest for decades, leaving whole generations of students and teachers numbly indifferent or blind to the value of great literature and a much smaller minority to discover that value for themselves without benefit of lecture or newsprint.

The task of literary criticism is to discuss and reveal the strengths and virtues, the flaws or weaknesses, of any given literary work, in language that is intelligible to the literate and well-read student or layman. Reason employed in the pursuit of truth about any literary work ought to be a clearly understood and accepted basis for any discussion of literature. That it is not, and has not been for a very long time, is shamefully evident in virtually every college or university literature course, or in almost any book on the subject. The abandonment and even derision of reason and humanist values, and the substitution of semantics, subjectivism, "deconstructionism," and sociology have not only divorced literary criticism from our culture, but suborned literature itself, to such an extent that the detective novel has become virtually the sole surviving pocket of Western literature.

It is the purpose of this essay to present an overview of how modern criticism is now assaulting this last bastion of the plotted novel, and to demonstrate that what was done to the "serious" novel, poetry, and drama, is now being done to the detective or mystery genre. For a first rate and clear discussion of the destruction wrought by modern criticism, I refer the reader to Peter Shaw's *The War Against the Intellect,* and especially his chapter "Literary Criticism" (University of Iowa Press, 1989).

While I have a dozen complaints against modern literary criticism, I shall touch on only the principal ones, which are: 1) that many literary critics view the detective fiction genre as a vehicle through which to propound or vent their usually dark views of Western, and in particular, American, culture; 2) that in modern literary criticism, there is an undeniable, and undenied, political theme, predominantly collectivist, often Marxist or leftist, invariably cloaked in sociological terms; and 3) that while the political nature of modern literary criticism is rooted in an ostensive concern for "the masses,, "the common man," "egalitarianism," and other "anti-elitist" dogma, it is for the most part the exclusive preserve of theorists who have rendered it virtually unintelligible to all but themselves.

The body of literature which comprises literary criticism of solely the detective fiction genre is huge and outwardly daunting, but it faithfully mirrors in tone and content the much larger corpus of the field. Except in a few instances, my observations will be limited to what has been said about the detective fiction genre or about specific examples of it.

I should find it ironic that a genre one of whose fundamental tenet is the validity of objective knowledge should be the subject of so much study and analysis by exponents of a school of philosophy that denies it. But, I do not. Our culture is governed by a bewildering and tenacious irrationality. It was inevitable that the genre should attract the attention of modern literacy criticism. I wonder if many of the genre's practitioners who once pined for "serious" literary acknowledgment do not now regret the smile "from above." What was inimical to other levels of literature is doubly so to detective fiction. But before wading into any of these issues, some space should be devoted to definitions, or at least to the definition of detective fiction.

As a definition of a detective story, "tales of ratiocination" has always seemed to me inadequate, and later definitions do not embrace all the varieties that have evolved since Poe's time. The *Oxford Universal Dictionary* (1955) defines a detective as "one whose occupation it is to discover matters artfully concealed."

But what kinds of matters? What things may be "artfully concealed," and by whom, so that a story could be called a "crime" story? *Men* conceal things from other *men:* their identities, their intentions, their motives, thoughts, and responsibility for certain actions. Often the concealment takes the form of a crime, i.e., an immoral action perpetrated against another; in the case of murder, the act of concealment is directed at the

137

living. Thus a detective's occupation is the discovery and resolution of a crime. Reason, or ratiocination, and *only reason,* enables him to uncover clues, establish evidence, infer motives, build and test hypotheses, and ultimately identify the perpetrator. A story that employs ESP, "intuition" or inexplicable insight, or any other method that bypasses reason and man's cognitive faculty, is not a true detective story, but a fraud wearing the genre's trench coat.

But it is a *moral* conflict which sets a detective story in motion. Moral conflicts necessitate value judgments of right and wrong, of good and evil, by both an author and his characters. A detective can only think and take action on evidence, which may be physical clues or others' actions. Thoughts that do not result in criminal action are not evil thoughts; nor are they evidence, not even when they are spoken or articulated (except in special circumstances, such as in a confession or other form of statement of culpability). Except in totalitarian societies, thoughts cannot be punished, and in any society unexpressed thoughts cannot be known or proven. Only an action, or the physical residue of an action, can be validly admitted as proof of intent or commission.

Here I introduce Ayn Rand's statement about detective fiction, which is that it "presents, in simple, primitive essentials, the conflict of good and evil; that is the root of its appeal." [1] This names a detective story's fundamental moral suasion and focus. Within a moral context, a detective story is a demonstration of the art of evidentiary reasoning. Fights, gun play, chases, and seductions are optional, but if they are featured in a story, they must have a purpose, which is to add a value to the extended syllogism that a detective story follows from the beginning to the end.

So a detective story – hard-boiled or soft, locked room or well-mannered murder, police procedural or amateur sleuth-may be defined as that category of fiction whose *principal* moral conflict causes or is the result of criminal acts, which are resolved by the art of reasoning. I stress *principal* because it specifies a detective story's central or governing motif. Stories that include a detective story subplot are not strictly detective stories, though often the resolution of a major plot will hinge in some way on the resolution of a minor detective story plot. The definition also excludes any story in which a criminal act is not a key determining factor in a story's plot or resolution. I believe this definition is both broad and specific enough to subsume all the varieties of detective fiction.

As for the appeal of detective fiction mentioned by Rand, and contrary to all the cumbersome and often bizarre explanations for it that occur in modern criticism, Jacques Barzun has best expressed the draw of detective fiction and the cause of its enduring popularity:

"Detection is *par excellence* the romance of reason."[2]

Barzun's is one of the most eloquent statements on the value of reason. He implies that there is something glorious about man's capacity for it. Absent from his statement is any nuance of the common premise that reason is a cold, impersonal, unloving imposition. That he chose to say "romance," instead of "story" or "tale," reveals a profound respect for man's mind and a belief that rationality is one of his most exciting attributes.

In violent contrast to Barzun's position is the recurrent condescension accorded the genre by the critical establishment. This is often thickly veiled or tiredly patronizing. Even many of those critics who do not explicitly assault the genre feel bound to sneer at it from beneath their prose, or to mask their praise under a patina of apology.

It is necessary that the intelligentsia would treat the genre as an anathema, and the attention it is getting today would not have been imaginable a few decades ago. Then, even academics and professional critics needed something to turn to for relief from a cultural malaise they inculcated and sustained. Apparently someone realized that this form of popular literature contradicted the culture. The nest was not their own, but it had to be fouled, too. Commenting on this paradox, Helmut Heissenbuttel, a German critic and essayist, wrote that "the crime novel is something which is missed by so many critics of modern literature, namely, legitimate reading matter for all. Everyone can feel at home in it." Heissenbuttel ended this observation with what cannot be construed as a compliment to his colleagues: "The critics, to be sure, seem unhappy about just this."[3]

Robin Winks, a professor of history at Yale and probably the best scholar of the genre in this country, observed that "the more complicated the cultural artifact, the happier the literary critic, and the more abstracted from any genuine understanding of precisely how detective fiction functions in society he becomes."[4] (Elsewhere, Winks makes the unwarranted and presumptuous remark that "good mystery novelists are quite conscious of the quality of parody in their work."[5]) In an observation about critics that cuts across all genres, Henri Peyre wrote, long before detective fiction criticism became respectable or fashionable, that critics write "with a note of bitterness at their isolation and of self-righteous pride at differing from the Philistine who does not know what he ought to like and for what reason."[6]

In the introduction to the *Catalogue of Crime,* Barzun noted that "the evolution of crime fiction (meaning all the current varieties) has since 1930 accurately reflected the social mood and the catchwords of each succeeding decade. Indeed, every four or five years the tone changes and the illustrative characters and actions follow the prevailing attitude of Western man toward his world."[7] This is no less true of modern literary criticism, except that the direction and purpose of modern criticism has remained consistent. Only the vocabularies change.

To contrast the kinds of interpretation put on detective fiction, let us examine three different commentaries on Dashiell Hammett's *The Maltese Falcon.* Here are novelist Ross Macdonald's remarks on both the story and its "symbol," the statuette of the falcon. Hammett's story is "a fable of modern man in quest of love and money.... The black bird is hollow.... Probably Hammett intended the ultimate worthlessness of the black bird to be more than a bad joke on his protagonist. I see it as a symbol of a lost tradition."[8]

Even though I disagree with his appraisal, I have no objection to it, chiefly because Macdonald offers it as a considered opinion, as speculation on the meaning of the story. He does not claim that Hammett meant the story or the statuette to stand for anything specific, nor does he insist that we accept his interpretation as an iron-clad verity. He has no information which confirms the author's expressed intentions. Macdonald more or less describes the story, and makes one factual statement. The rest is acknowledged hypothesis.

T. J. Binyon, a critic and lecturer at Oxford and also a novelist, writes on the character of Sam Spade. "The reader cannot empathize with him or vicariously experience his fear or excitement or pain. And at times the careful, pedantic precision of Hammett's style seems to lapse into self-parody, as in his description of Spade making a midnight snack: 'He spread liverwurst on, or cold corned beef between, the small ovals of bread he had sliced.'"[9]

Here again is an instance of a critic merely offering an opinion of an author's work, and not a notation of fact. Binyon does not assert that Hammett lapses into self-parody; he qualifies a credible hypothesis with "seems to," because he does not know Hammett's motive to choosing to include a "realist" episode such as depicting Spade fixing a sandwich.

Binyon accurately evaluates Spade's character and Hammett's writing style in terms that are intelligible to the reader.

An extreme instance of a more common practice is Steven Marcus' treatment of the Hammett novel. Discussing the many ways in it in which Hammett "represents the world of crime as a reproduction of the modern capitalist society that it depends on," and Hammett's supposed literary method of accomplishing them, Marcus writes that "one of them ... is the Maltese Falcon itself, which turns out to be and contains within itself the history of capitalism. It is originally a piece of plunder, part of what Marx called the 'primitive accumulation...'"[10]

Marcus' assertion deserves not only a critique, but a historical correction. First, as one can see, his statement is not qualified as is Macdonald's or Binyon's. Hammett may indeed have intended the Maltese Falcon to be a symbol of something; if he had, surely the intention would have surfaced in his papers. And Marcus may have felt that he had legitimate license to presume that the author meant the statuette to mean what he, Marcus, claims it to mean; after all, Hammett's left-wing associations are a matter of record, and much of his other fiction is colored by an arguably watered-down Marxist "realism."

But if Hammett had meant the statuette to stand for something, then why an exclusively *political* idea? For also present in *The Maltese Falcon,* and in the rest of Hammett's work, is a tone of cynicism, of a tired relinquishment of idealism and moral values, which phenomenon is not inherently tethered to any particular political conviction or ideology. The depiction of a partial or wholesale uncorrected lapse of values in any novel, genre or mainstream, results in the creation of a sense of helplessness or sad ineffectuality in a story's protagonist, who is placed in a milieu that then seems overtly hostile, indifferent, or insensible to him and to what he professes is the good. A "hero" with such abbreviated convictions must settle for inconsequential victories and a gnawing certainty that the world is evil. A better example than Hammett's Sam Spade of this "hardboiled" view is Raymond Chandler's Philip Marlowe, who, precisely because of his "knightly" values and his limited success in achieving them, has been virtually canonized by the doyens of the genre.

If there *must* be an explanation of the statuette's vaunted symbolism, I believe the added line of dialogue at the end of John Huston's faithful 1941 film of the novel marvelously sums up Hammett's core metaphysics and epistemology. The line so distills the story's gray determinist atmosphere and its near-sighted pragmatism that I think it is as close to the author's true intent as one can get without actually asking him. Spade is about to follow the police out after they have arrested Brigid O'Shaughnessy.

His friend on the force, Tom Polhaus, picks up the statuette and asks what it is. "The stuff dreams are made of," replies Spade, taking it. That line (paraphrased from a speech by Prospero in *The Tempest)* is so appropriate, and so captures the essence of Hammett's view of existence, that it is a disappointment *not* to encounter it in the novel itself. But the sentiment behind it is not the exclusive, unique perspective of existentialists or Marxists. Capitalists, cowboys, and, I imagine, even a few popes, have expressed it, too, in fiction and in fact, with the same pathos.

The historical correction concerns Marcus' association of "capitalism" with "plunder." It completely ignores the statuette's history as related by Casper Gutman. As that character (and, let us not forget, Hammett) tells it, the story is neither in fact an early episode of capitalism, nor was it intended as one. The Knights of Rhodes, who purportedly had the statuette made for Holy Roman Emperor Charles V of Spain, were not "capitalists." While the Crusades, *sub rosa,* "were largely a matter of loot," this particular organization began as a charitable community in Jerusalem, founded by more or less sincere knights, but it later grew to become an independent military force and a rival of the Knights Templars. The Templars were repressed in the fourteenth century and much of their wealth and lands were given by the Church to the Knights of Rhodes (or the Hospitallers). The organization acquired its fabulous holdings chiefly through grants and bequests from feudal barons in Europe, who gave to save their souls. In fact, it was Pope Clement V of Avignon who recognized the Knights' right to occupy Rhodes and Malta; Charles V of Spain may or may not have made any decisions concerning the Knights' status on Malta, but he did not appear until early in the sixteenth century.

Neither feudal Europe nor Renaissance Europe can be characterized as "capitalist"; the largest accumulations of wealth were for centuries held by the Church, monarchs, and countless lesser rulers. The Knights of Rhodes managed to increase the value of their holdings over time, in addition to maintaining hospitals and fighting Turkish and Moslem incursions in the Mediterranean and later the corsairs.

The Mediterranean of the sixteenth century *did* spawn the infancy of capitalism, and no doubt the Knights' holdings allowed them to play a small part in it. But the ships that sailed in and out of the Italian ports were financed or owned largely by traders, bankers, and investors-not by medieval plunderers or their heirs. Capitalism creates and distributes wealth, not destroys, loots, or hoards it. The value of the created wealth actually plundered by Algerian pirates from those ships was infinitely greater than any that could be assigned to the original, jewel-encrusted Maltese Falcon, had it ever existed.

Hammett insinuates neither Marcus' interpretation nor any other modern critical "reading," nor even my own. In the entire novel, there is not one political or ideological allusion, suggestion, or cryptonym.

We can understand Marcus' position a little better if we read what he has to say about Hammett's "Flitcraft" fable and the moral of this digression in the novel. "For here we come upon the unfathomable and most mysteriously irrational part of it all, how despite everything we have learned and everything we know, men will persist in behaving and trying to behave sanely, rationally, sensibly, and responsibly. And we will continue to persist even when we know that there is no logical or metaphysical, no discoverable or demonstrable reason for doing so." [11]

I am not certain of the purpose of Spade's Flitcraft digression. Perhaps Hammett meant it to be Spade's circumlocutious warning to Brigid O'Shaughnessy about his future behavior. (If there was a point to Spade's telling her the Flitcraft fable, she did not get it.) I call it a digression because there is no further reference to it in the novel, and that episode and Spade's encounter with Rhea Gutman are not well integrated in the story.[12] If anything substantive can be said about the fable, it is that it anticipates existentialism with its mixed elements of pragmatism and fallibilism. In the novel's penultimate chapter, Spade expresses a distinctly Kantian ethic ("When a man's partner is killed he's supposed to do something about it"), which is qualified by a distinctly pragmatist ethic ("it's bad business to let the killer get away with it"), which in turn is qualified by a determinist non-ethic ("expecting me to run criminals down and then let them go is like asking a dog to catch a rabbit and let it go").

Which is root and which is branch – Spade's Flitcraft fable or his reasons for turning O'Shaughnessy in – is a moot point here. Hammett's Sam Spade exudes a blending of these bleak philosophies throughout the novel. This may help to explain why he has fascinated so many modern critics.[12]

Marcus' approving commentary on the Flitcraft fable exhibits deep existentialist and deconstructionist roots: existentialist, because it expresses the view that rationality is pointless or futile (to behave rationally is evidence of "irrationality"; as a contradiction and a premise, it expresses the view that rationality is pointless or futile (to behave rationally is evidence of "irrationality"; as a contradiction and a premise, it might be true if one's sole premise was that death is the only absolute in life; one wonders if Marcus brakes for red lights); deconstructionist, because Marcus' obvious hostility to capitalism permits him to indulge in one of what J. Hillis Miller, a leading advocate of "free play" critical interpretation, might call "endless commentaries." [13]

Marcus has either genuinely misread *The Maltese Falcon* – a likelihood I strongly doubt – or consciously "misread" it for his own ends.

Arthur Quiller-Couch, the English author and scholar, emphasized that the "first obligation we owe to any classic ... is to treat it *absolutely:* not for any secondary or derivative purpose, or purpose recommended as useful by any manual: but at first solely to interpret the meaning its author intended: that in short we should *trust* any given masterpiece for its operation and on others."[14]

This credo, with its implicit demand for intellectual honesty, is not one that is recognized by (or perhaps not even comprehensible to) most modern critics. Steven Marcus is certainly not alone in dismissing, ignoring, or inventing an author's "intended" meaning to suit his own purposes, and I cite his treatment of Hammett's work as one of innumerable instances of the practice.

"A growing tendency during the last fifty years to question the value of technology and ratiocination," writes Elliot L. Gilbert, an authority on the genre, "has made the theme of the failed detective a prominent one in the works of recent writers not usually associated with the genre of mystery fiction." Citing works by contemporary French authors, Gilbert observes that "all see in the limitations of detection a metaphor for a culture that has exhausted the possibilities of rationalism .... [N]ovelists, playwrights, and filmmakers ... employ the figure of the detective in their work to symbolize the arrogance of any search for final truth. On the other hand, traditional mystery fiction, in a wide variety of forms, continues to thrive."[15]

But for how long? Arrayed against the genre are the literary and esthetic branches of a philosophy inimical to the nature and identity of detective fiction. If I have stressed the elements of existentialism and deconstructionism, it is because if these and similar ideas have any consequences (if not an actual purpose), it is to emasculate the genre of its means, purpose, and especially of its value as a *life-affirming* art.

If the genre's means is the extended syllogism, if its purpose is to demonstrate in romantic fiction the efficacy of the human mind, and if its value to the reader is a special affirmation of that efficacy in realms other than in his own life, what else can be the aim of their antipodes but to destroy or discredit reason, to denigrate or negate the mind, and to estrange men from their values, from themselves, and even from each other by "proving" how irrational, futile, and desolate is man's existence?

"From the first Hammett was admired by critics who did not particularly like the detective story formula," writes James Naremore. To them "the solution to the murder [was] less important than the depiction of a *milieu.*"[16] Calling the hardboiled detective novel a "valuable and interesting form," George Grella asserts that "it presents a worthy alternative to the thriller of manners, and indicates the potency and durability of the national cultural vision, the American Dream, as it constantly metamorphoses into nightmare."[17]

And Erik Routley, in a vividly open attack on the genre, writes that the moral case against detective fiction is "that the detective story is the product and the weapon of a middle class puritan society whose morality makes claims that have no foundation."[18] Among those "foundationless" claims, celebrated and "perpetuated" by detective stories, are "the acceptance of assumptions about law and order," "the rights of property," the "sanctity of human life," and the "propriety of the punishment of wrongdoers."[19] Ernest Mandel also indicts detective fiction as an instrument of class oppression. "Crime never pays. Bourgeois legality, bourgeois values, bourgeois society, always triumph in the end....Bourgeois rationality is a cheater's rationality."[20] These pronouncements steal the thunder from Edmund Wilson's persnickety dismissal of detective fiction as "wasteful of time and degrading to the intellect."[21]

Articulate, contrary arguments in favor or in defense of detective fiction are rarer and divisive. The "pro" side of the debate lacks the "solidarity" of the side that views the genre through purely sociological or ideological lenses. Novelist Dorothy Sayers, for all her passionate devotion to it, still declared that "the detective story is part of the literature of escape, and not of expression."[22]

In a more recent essay, Aaron Marc Stein takes the position that the detective novel is just as legitimate a means of expression as the non-genre novel. "Artists select whatever aspect or segment of the actual world they choose to explore and celebrate," he writes. In creating an imaginary world, "a successful work of art has something to say about actuality and reality. The choice made by the detective story writers was the exploration and celebration of the process of inductive reasoning."[23]

W. H. Auden, in his famous essay, "The Guilty Vicarage," viewed the detective novel's chief value as a cathartic experience, in which a reader's doubts about his moral worth are expiated."I suspect that the typical reader of detective stories is ... a person who suffers from a sense of sin.... To have a sense of sin means to feel guilty at there being an ethical choice to make, a guilt which, however 'good' I may become, remains unchanged."[24] In radical opposition to Auden is J. Kenneth Van Dover. Discussing the symbiotic rapport between authors and readers of popular literature, including detective and suspense fiction, Van Dover contends that the implicit format "accepts the intuitions of its readers and arranges them in a straightforward drama that proves the world does proceed in an orderly fashion- that there is an intelligible plot concealed in current events, that character is knowable, that good and evil are definite opposites, and that we are good." In Van Dover's company has appeared lately novelist and critic William L. DeAndrea, who has rejected "a call for the end of the hero" in detective fiction by many of the genre's practitioners, and enunciated some fundamental but much neglected assumptions. The mystery story, he writes, is "the literature of moral choice," a "celebration of reason and courage,"[25] and an affirmation of "individual worth and responsibility" and of "the principle of private property"– "especially the ultimate in private property, a person's life."[26]

But the predominant schools of modern literary criticism – phenomenology, reader-response and other variants of Structuralism, the New Criticism, and all the variants of deconstructionism – can hardly celebrate reason or aver that character is knowable, when they share the conclusion that since objective reality cannot be known, neither can any given literary work. At this point, most critics split between those who claim that a work can be known by employing *non-rational* means or by attending to external or nonessential factors associated with it, and those who claim that a work cannot be known at all, but that close analyses of it will produce an infinite chain of differentiated meanings.

To Immanuel Kant modern criticism owes not only the premise of the impossibility of objective knowledge, but also the idea of "esthetic distance" (as opposed to "esthetic involvement," or a concern with a story's characters or structure). To Georg W. F. Hegel it owes chiefly both the idea that reality is a creation of the mind, and the mechanics of thesis, antithesis, and synthesis. And from Martin Heidegger it inherited the method of phenomenology, in which all Aristotelian methods are discarded in a search for a thing's "essence" **or** "meaning," and the death fetishism of existentialism. Historically, these schools have been opponents; but none of the contributing ideas that underlie modern literary criticism is fundamentally antithetical to the others in means or ends.

If you innocently remarked at a Critics' Tea Party (Lewis Carroll might have appreciated the predicament) that a particular novel was well written, admirably plotted, a delight to read, and a noteworthy example of detective fiction, your other guests would not let you get away with it. One group would insist that the work be judged and defined by such things as the author's childhood bout with chicken pox, by the socio-economic circumstances of his family, and by how those and other societal factors also influenced the content, structure, and style of his novel.

Another group of critics would elaborate on *your* childhood diseases

and family's socio-economic status, and claim that your response to or evaluation of the novel was indelibly branded by those and other factors about yourself over which you have no control, and that, in any event, such a "simplistic" estimate as yours can hardly qualify as a "serious" reading, since your superficial report indicates an obvious blindness to all the layers of textual implications in the novel.

One or another faction of a third group may or may not agree

with the first two, but proceed to analyze your "reading" or "misreading" and to judge whether or not the novel's textual "aporia" contained valid sets of "signifiers" and "signifieds," then hazard a guess that its "traces" were nominally miscued and a little tricky to detect (so you can be forgiven that, at least), but then conclude that your "strategy" was all

147

wrong – no, *inappropriate* since there is no "wrong" or "right" way to read or "misread" a text. The other faction very likely will agree with the first, but add that more readings or "misreadings" are needed to better substantiate the text's full complement of dispersed contradictions.

But long before the third group enters the dialogue, you *and* the novel are already out of the picture. And you have not even heard yet from the gynocritics and the phallocentrists.

This is what has descended on the detective fiction genre. The phenomenon is not limited to that genre, of course, but is the norm in the whole field of modern criticism. It filters down from the universities and tests positive in the most unlikely wells.

Julian Symons, for example, writing on the success of Ian Fleming's James Bond novels and why they attracted such a wide readership, notes that in "the fifties, readers responded to Bond because he provided an excitement lacking in their lives." This is a fair and very credible explanation. But then he goes on to claim that into "the British post-war atmosphere of virtuous Puritanism he brought a celebration of physical pleasures, including those of sadism and masochism."[27] Symons maligns both the Bond novels and their readers, implying that anyone who values an exciting romantic hero is *de facto* a latent pervert, especially if the hero undertakes great risks and endures brutal treatment at the hands of his country's enemies.

On Fleming again, Tony Bennett and Janet Woollacott explain that while "relating the Bond novels to Fleming as their extra-textual origin and the source of their meaning, the ways in which such relations have been constructed have differed from those in evidence in critical discourses where the author function is more fully developed."[28] This means, I think, that there is good reason to suspect that Fleming was writing fiction, and not a disguised autobiography. Lawmakers, when they want to put over questionable legislation, usually say it with statistics. Modern critics, when they seek to exercise an expensively and assiduously acquired argot, usually say it with sophistry.

I would say that a detective story's clues must not be strewn randomly or arbitrarily throughout a plot, but have legitimate places in the logical sequence of events that is a plot. Dennis Porter, however, would rather put it this way: "More obviously than other narrative genres, the detective novel promotes the myth of the necessary chain. It implies that the only path to the destination that is the solution of a mystery is the step-by-step path of logico-temporal reconstruction."[29]

This almost makes sense on the first pass, but one or two rereadings are needed to make sure it means what one may suspect it means. Read one way, it may strike one as a convoluted way of reiterating what I said about clues. One might then ask oneself why Porter felt it necessary to say it the way he did, and probably conclude that the statement is an instance of "padding." On this subject, Ernest Gowers remarked in *Plain Words* that "padding can only be defined as the use of words, phrases and even sentences that contribute nothing to the reader's perception of the writer's meaning. [30]

But is this a genuine instance of padding? On the surface, yes, and on that level it not only contributes nothing to the reader's comprehension, but actually subtracts from his understanding and introduces a sense of doubt. This is because other, extra-contextual meanings seem to be appended to the words in it. What does Porter mean by a "necessary chain," why is it a "myth," and why does a detective novel "promote" it? Why is a "solution" a "destination," and why must it be reached by a "path"? Finally, what is a "logico-temporal reconstruction"?

One could rephrase Porter's statement this way: The detective novel by its nature subscribes to (or "promotes") the idea (or "myth") that problems can be solved only by syllogisms (if *A,* then *B;* if *B,* then C ...), and that the job of a detective is to recreate or comprehend the essential factors of a crime. Thus a syllogism, or the causo-connective link between things or actions, becomes a "necessary chain," which must be followed "step-by-step" to a "logico-temporal reconstruction," which means a rational answer to the question. All this, asserts Porter, is a "myth" that must be sustained in the fictive world of a reader's imagination, and has few referents in the world outside the story; out there, cause and effect and answers to questions are apparently superstitions which cannot be sustained. The key word in his statement, *myth,* not only seems to justify the awkward syntax by allying itself with the other curiously used words, but implies that to address a reader's *rationality* – i.e.., his expectation of provable causo-connections-is just another arbitrary way of telling a story, one which happens to pander to a reader's naiveté.

But what of the novels of Victor Hugo and Feodor Dostoyevsky, or of the plays of Friedrich Schiller, Henrik Ibsen, or Terence Rattigan, or even of the short stories of Rudyard Kipling? Do not the plots in these and in other great works *very* obviously "promote" the "myth" of a "necessary chain" –

the absence of which would reduce them to the level of most contemporary "serious" literature?

If the epithet "talking heads" has been earned by any current field of intellectual inquiry, literary criticism has won it. The authors of most published studies in literary criticism do not address the reading public, even though their titles may be found in commercial as well as in university bookstores, but rather their peers in the practice. Forgotten is the hesitant student or layman, who on one hand might feel intellectually inadequate for not being able to instantly grasp what is said by others with carefree abandon, but who on the other may wistfully agree with Peyre that "if obscurity there be, it should be up to the critics to dispel it."[31] Peyre was speaking of the obscurity to be found in much literature and art. However, the field of literary criticism has itself nearly vanished into what seems a thick fog of swirling nomenclatures. Strange sounds emanate from it, but the otherwise competent lay mind cannot decipher them. There is a background noise, low and constant, which he may be aware of. It is nothing but the drone of a fog-making machine.

"In their anxiety to avoid the deluge of snappy vulgarisms," wrote Peyre, "into which authors of popular articles on literature believe they must plunge, scholarly critics have erected barriers of 'objective correlatives,' 'organicity,' and medical and psychological jargon at the door of their sanctum."[32] Since he wrote those words in 1949, the lexiconic barricade has been piled higher with such unwieldy obstructions as "intertextualiry," intratextuality," "subject-vortex," "infinite regressions," "deferred significations," "totemic systems," "unfoldings," and, of course, "myths."

Robert Alter, a leading critic of the linguistics analysis school, reveals that the barricade is purposeful and that the task of dispelling obscurity – their own or that found in literary works – is not one most modern critics are keen to shoulder."The prospect of a value-free study of literature is positively consoling after the apparent failure of engaged criticism as an ideal," he writes."The formidable intellectual apparatus of Structuralism ... lends it a particularly powerful attraction as a method of studying literature without the old embarrassing concerns of value; for it offers the literary intelligentsia what any professional or priestly caste needs in order to maintain its own coherence and morale – an esoteric language, a set of elaborate procedures that can be performed only by the initiate, and the conviction that the specialized rituals of the caste have universal efficacy, or at least universal applicability."[33]

The Structuralists are not the sole school of literary criticism with an "esoteric" language or a set of "elaborate procedures." In fact, all schools of human endeavor have these things, from schools of philosophy to schools of auto repair. The test is whether or not the "language" and the "procedures" have any legitimate bearing on the subject.

Coincidently, Alter confirms an important phenomenon noted by Ortega y Gasser, of a reversal, in the nineteenth century, of the Aristotelian premise in metaphysics from *operari sequitur esse* – *actions* follow, and derive from, being, to *esse sequitur operari* – *the* being of a thing is nothing bur the sum total of its actions and function.[34] Alter restates it when he observes that in "the Structuralist view, *homo sapiens* is effectively replaced by what Jonathan Culler [a leading Structuralist theorist] has aptly called *'homo significans,* maker and reader of signs.' The epistemological shift is crucial: in this approach there are no discernible 'objects' of knowledge in human experience, only signs to be interpreted, and hence man can no longer be defined as the knower."[35]

Denis Donoghue, Henry James Professor of Letters at New York University, commenting on the aims of post-Structuralists, notes that "they replace the author by language itself, which is then studied as an impersonal system, a system that doesn't need a person to work it.... [N]othing in language corresponds to the identity of a person or to his apparent continuity from one moment to the next ....The author is at best a secretary, a scribe." Structuralist readers, on the other hand, "are urged to adopt an ironic or skeptical attitude toward whatever they read; they are to know that it is poisoned." "The task of modern criticism" for the Structuralists, says Donoghue, "is to document the extent to which the modern languages have been corrupted."[36]

What bearing could any of this have on detective fiction genre criticism? For one thing, both the reversal of man in the scheme of things and the hyper-specialized, "talking heads" self-insulation of modern criticism not only complement each other, but have over the decades combined to permeate our culture deeply enough that it has begun to affect the genre itself, which was once thought to be immune to literary fashions. A number of detective novels have appeared in which the detective's state of mind, innocence or guilt is more important than the case he is investigating. Often the detective ends up questioning the evidence of his senses and his concepts of right and wrong. Some of these novels are interesting, but they too closely crowd the line dividing genre from mainstream fiction.

Many are blundering attempts to be "serious"; their authors have left the public behind and chosen to "write up" to the critics instead. Still others seek to emulate the Georges Simenon school of detection by evoking the milieu of the criminal and replacing objective judgment with subjective "certainty." And there has been renewed interest in the *noir* genre of such writers as Cornell Woolrich, Jim Thompson, and Paul Cain. Long on the fringes of detective fiction literature, this genre's deadening "realism," gutter and kitchen sink view of man, and ambient malevolence appear to be natural draws for writers to whom the value-negating quandaries of criminals, psychotics, and recidivists represent a Golconda of literary ore.

Even critics who do not wish to burden the genre with "readings," "misreadings," or other insubstantial evaluations feel compelled to try their hands at "serious" criticism. In an otherwise perceptive discussion of Raymond Chandler's novels, Jerry Speir, commenting on an exchange between Philip Marlowe and Harry Jones, a minor character in *The Big Sleep,* writes that "Harry has exceeded the bounds of intelligible language. But in that very fact lies Chandler's point, that language is but a poor reflection of the complexity of which the mind is capable. And, paradoxically, even the language of Harry Jones can launch us beyond our normal perceptions simply by disregarding our learned expectations."[37]

Chandler meant nothing of the kind. He was simply writing good dialogue and *counting* on our "normal perceptions" and "learned expectations" to let us know what Harry Jones was talking about.

There is nothing else to be spun out of Jones's grammatically mangled statement, which is simply a stylized observation on the quirks of memory.[38] It neither "exceeds" the bounds of intelligibility, nor

"reflects" any wider epistemological ramifications. But Speir contradicts himself when he ascribes the "point" to Chandler. Earlier, he states that Chandler eschewed "intellectualism" in his writing and wrote in the genre because it was "clearly defined and unadulterated by any political or intellectual forays."[39] If this is true, then Chandler was not trying to make a point about language. Speir might have done well to heed Chandler's own dictum concerning critics: "Good critical writing is measured by the perception and evaluation of the subject; bad critical writing by the necessity of maintaining the professional standing of the critic."[40] In other words, to root for deeper meanings in an author's narrative or dialogue where none is intended or indicated, is to excavate a hole the author himself did not think digging.[41]

Still other critics write about the "classics" of the genre as though they were examples of contemporary trends in detective fiction."Detective stories," writes James Naremore, "are the most fetishistic of literary genres because the trivial objects of the investigation – the 'clues' function like the over-determined symbols in dreams." Elsewhere, Naremore, commenting on Dashiell Hammett's "neutral" technique of the third-person narrative, states that it "makes Spade a technician, brooding on the fine points of a problem, but it also displaces the traditional ratiocinative values of detective fiction in

favor of another quality that was always inherent in the formal representation of the surface of things."[42] "The Op may catch the real thief or collar the actual crook," writes Steven Marcus about another of Hammett's characters, the Continental Op, but "that is not entirely the point .... What Hammett has done ... is to include as part of the contingent and dramatic consciousness of his narrative the circumstance chat the work of the detective is itself a fiction-making activity, a discovery or creation by fabrication of something new in the world, or hidden, latent, potential, or as yet undeveloped within it....The story as a whole is an exercise in disambiguation ...."[43]

There could be no doubt about the suasion of such interpretations in detective fiction criticism when, for example, Vincent B. Leitch's representation of another critic's position could serve as their model. Chiding fellow theorist M. H. Abrams for some (unintelligible) reservations about the consequences of deconstructionist practice, Leitch observes that the "death of the self of the reader and the undecidability of the text produced the demise of meaning: in place of reader, text, and meaning were vortex, abyss, and infinite regress."[44] Leitch nowhere else attempts a reply to Abrams' charge; his unqualified assessment of it stands in mute but (in comparison to Abrams) intelligible acknowledgment.

What else could be left for modern critics to say when, on one hand, novelist Walker Percy calls contemporary "serious" novels "diagnostic," but then admits indifference to the fate of literature's "traditional baggage"– plot, characterization, description, setting, and narrative?"...[I]f the practitioners of the *nouveau roman"* manage to discard these things, "it is all right with me-if it works."[45] Or, on the other hand, when Ralph Harper asks: "...[D]o we think that life is so difficult that the crises of thrillers fairly represent our inner responses to it? There are no final answers here. If nobody knows me, neither do I know myself."[46] Such a statement is not just a rhetorical expression of "esthetic distance"; nor is the denial of the possibility of "final answers" just an apparent invitation to more "endless commentaries." It is a confession that the "text" is not the only victim of a deconstructionist's prying crowbar; if the reader's "self" was impervious to such an assault, such an admission would not be possible.

What, indeed, could be left for the author of a *nouveau roman policier* to say, if he chooses to displace ratiocinative values with representing the surfaces of things and discards all the traditional baggage, and puts his gumshoed manqué through the motions of fetish-chasing, fiction-making, fabrication and disambiguation, in pursuit of bourgeois justice and forever elusive inner responses? If his premise is that a criminal is merely the "sum of his actions and function," with little or no element of volition governing his equation, then his criminal will be a mere sociological phenomenon, presumably beyond moral judgment.

And if his detective is ruled by the same formula, then he, too, will be a prisoner of predetermination, reduced to reading "signs," lamenting the ontological corners he and his prey have been painted into by their "beings," and anguishing over or cursing the necessity of making moral judgments. Questions of innocence and guilt become superfluous, as do the victim and the crime, except as they are used to sabotage or disintegrate the concepts of guilt and innocence, of victim and crime, and even of rationality.

And to the modern literary critic, whether he is reporting the minute, artificial profundities of that kind of "detective" novel, or burying clean simplicity under pages of abstruse complexities of his own invention, all the genre's defining attributes are but pretentious embellishments otherwise known as "necessary chains," "author functions," "destinations," and "myths." These and other hyperbolic terms permit him to discuss everything about a detective story but its essentials; too often they permit him to "reveal" things which are not in the story at all.

There are other aspects of detective fiction criticism which cannot be discussed at length here but nevertheless deserve mention. One is the ways in which modern criticism, especially as it has been encountered by students in college and university literature studies, has helped to drive away many Americans from even minimal interest in great literature (or killed their budding interest in it), and abetted the anti-intellectual and anti-literary attitudes in our culture.

Horror stories of disgust and bewilderment seem to be the norm, and would be laughably satiric were they not so tragically real. Since the terms and methodologies of modern critical analysis are basically incommunicable to anyone who has not made a career of studying them, students who attend literature courses and who expect intelligibility from their instructors, must often resort to dishonest mimicry or second-guessing.

One acquaintance of mine related how, after a whole term of studying major Russian writers and wrestling unsuccessfully with what her linguistics analysis professor wanted his class to do with them, she handed in a thirty-page paper on Nikolai Gogol's *Dead Souls* in which she discussed, not the story, but, with inventive tongue-in-cheek, the significance of the *number* of sentences in each chapter's opening and closing paragraphs – and much to her surprise, was awarded the highest grade by her approvingly ecstatic professor. My point here is that accredited courses in mystery and detective fiction studies are now appearing in schools: will these genres be subjected to the same treatment, and share the fate of non-genre fiction?

Another aspect worth mentioning is the role of commercial or working critics of detective fiction. Commercial critics are less culpable than academic critics; the typical book reviewer for a newspaper or magazine *must* be intelligible, since his audience is the public. His criteria of what is good or bad detective fiction are very often as eclectic and arbitrary as those of his counterparts in academe, but frequently fair and objective. However, he is in the same cultural boat as is the reading public: he must take what is published and comment on it, according to his likes and talents.

He can neither influence literary trends nor cajole publishers or the public into favoring particular authors. His advice and recommendations more often than not go unheeded by the reading public. In fact, it would be fair to say that he almost invariably reports on authors whose works have already been discovered by the public; this is especially true of mystery and detective novels, as well as other thriller genres. Problems arise when the commercial critic begins to emulate the "talking heads" patois of his cloistered but more esteemed cousins in the universities.

It would be apropos to end here by citing the remarks of two well known authors of fiction on the subject of detective novels. The writers could not be farther apart in the scope of their work and in their fundamental outlooks, but I believe that, on this issue, they share the same dais. The basic characteristic of thrillers, including detective stories, "is *conflict,*" writes Ayn Rand, "which means: a clash of goals, which means:

purposeful action in pursuit of *values*. Thrillers are the product, the popular offshoot, of the *Romantic* school of art that sees man, not as a helpless pawn of fate, but as a being who possesses volition, whose life is directed by his own value-choices."[47] Popular literature, including detective fiction, "does not deal with abstract problems," and "does not raise or answer abstract questions; it assumes that man knows what he needs to know in order to live, and it proceeds to show his adventures in living (which is one of the reasons for its popularity among all types of readers, including the problem-laden intellectuals)."[48] Finally, as a branch of Romantic art, thrillers are experienced by writers and readers alike "simply as the desire to make life interesting."[49]

If this is true, then the goal of modern detective fiction criticism would seem to be, by most accounts, to raise abstract questions when there are none to be raised, to destroy or subvert the genre's value as an art, to deny or denigrate reason and volition, and to make life insensibly dull.

"It is the paradox of the mystery novel that while its structure will seldom if ever stand up under the close scrutiny of an analytical mind," writes Raymond Chandler, "it is precisely to that type of mind that it makes its greatest appeal." "All really good mysteries are reread, some of them many times. Obviously this would not happen if the puzzle were the only motive for the reader's interest. ... The mystery story must have color, lift, and a reasonable amount of dash."[50]

Towards the end of those same notes on the mystery novel, Chandler confidently, almost happily remarked that the "academicians have never got their dead hands on it." Sadly, he underestimated the appetite and goals of the modern critical mind, and its compulsion to maintain its professional standing at any cost. His presumption can be forgiven.

End Notes

1. Ayn Rand, *"The Girl Hunters,* by Mickey Spillane," *The Objectivist Newsletter* October 1962). 43.
2. Jacques Barzun, "Detection and Literature," *The Energies of Art* (1956; New York: Vintage Books, 1962), 307.
3. Helmut Heissenbuttel, "Rules of the Game of the Crime Novel," trans. by Glenn W. Most and William W. Stowe, *The Poetics of Murder: Detective Fiction and Literary Theory,* ed. Glenn W. Most and William W. Stowe (New York: Harcourt Brace Jovanovich, 1983), 205.
4. Robin W. Winks, Modus *Operandi: An Excursion Into Detective Fiction* (Boston: David R. Go dine, 1982), 111.
5. Robin W. Winks, Introduction, *Detective Fiction: Crime and Compromise,* ed. Dick Allen and David Chaco {New York: Harcourt Brace Jovanovich, 1974), 5·
6. Henri M. Peyre, "The Criticism of Contemporary Writing," *Lectures in Criticism,* Bollinger Series XVI (New York: Pantheon, 1949), 130.
7. Jacques Barzun, Introductory, A *Catalogue of Crime,* ed. Jacques Barzun and Wendell Hertig Taylor (New York: Harper & Row, 1971), n.
8. Ross Macdonald, "The Scene of the Crime," *Inward journey: Ross Macdonald,* ed. Ralph B. Sipper (1984; New York: The Mysterious Press, 1987), JI-) 2.
9. T. J. Binyon, 'Murder *Will Out: The Detective in Fiction* (Oxford: Oxford Univ. Press, 1989), 40-41.
10. Steven Marcus, "Dashiell Hammett," The *Poetics of Murder,* 205.
11. Ibid., 200-1.
12. The most likely explanation for the Flitcraft fable, the Rhea Gutman episode, and such naturalist episodes as Spade's fixing a sandwich, rolling a cigarette, or performing other actions that reflect what Binyon characterizes as Hammett's "careful, pedantic precision," is that *The Maltese Falcon* was originally serialized in *Black Mask* magazine in five installments in 1929-30. Hammett, then writing for the pulps, was paid for the number of words he produced. It also probably accounts for many of the novel's other incongruities not present in the Huston film (which is the most definitive of the three Hollywood versions-if by "definitive" we mean the truest and most accurate dramatization of a novel). Huston, working under the exigencies of another story-telling medium, cur much that was non-essential from the novel.
13. J. Hillis Miller, *The Linguistic Moment: From Wordsworth to Stevens* (Princeton: Princeton Univ. Press, 1985), 422.
14. Sir Arthur Quiller-Couch, "On the Use of Masterpieces," *On the Art of Reading* (Cambridge: Cambridge Univ. Press, 1920), 12-1313-
15. Elliot L. Gilbert, "Detective," *Dictionary of Literary Themes and Motifs,* 2 vols., ed. Jean-Charles Seigneuret (New York: Greenwood Press, 1988), 1:386.
16. James Naremore, "Dashiell Hammett and the Poetics of Hard-Boiled Detection," *Art in Crime Writing: Essays on Detective Fiction,* ed. Bernard Benstock (New York: St. Martin's Press, 1983), 63.
17. George Grella, "Murder and the Mean Streets," *Detective Fiction: Crime and Compromise,* 428.
18. Erik Routley, "The Case Against the Detective Story," *Detective Fiction: A Collection of Critical Essays.* ed. Robin W. Winks (1980; Woodstock: Foul Play Press, I988), I6J.

19.   Ibid., r64.
20.   Ernest Mandel, "A Marxist Interpretation of the Crime Story," *Detective Fiction: A Collection of Critical Essays,* 215-6
21.   Edmund Wilson, "Who Cares Who Killed Roger Ackroyd?" *Detective Fiction: A Collection of Critical Essays,* 39·
22.   Dorothy L. Sayers, Introduction, *The Omnibus of Crime* (Garden City: Garden City Publishing Co., 1929), 44.
23.   Aaron Marc Stein, "The Mystery Story in Cultural Perspective," *The Mystery Story, ed.* John
       Ball (San Diego: Univ. of California, 1976), 53.
24.   W H. Auden, "The Guilty Vicarage," *Detective Fiction: A Collection of Critical Essays,* 23-4.
25.   J. Kenneth Van Dover, *Murder in the Millions: Erie Stanley Gardner. Mickey Spillane. Ian Fleming(New* York: Frederick Ungar, 1984), 9.
26.   William L. DeAndrea, "J'Accuse!" *The Armchair Detective* 4 (1989), 371.
27.   Julian Symons, *Bloody Murder: From the Detective Story to the Crime Story* (1972; New York: Viking Penguin,
       1985), 223-24.
28.   Tony Bennett and Janet Woollacott, *Bond and Beyond: The Political Career of a Popular Hero* (New York: Methuen, 1987), 253.
29.   Dennis Porter, "Backward Construction and the Art of Suspense," *The Poetics of Murder, 333-334.*
30.   Sir Ernest Gowers, *Plain Words: A Guide to the Use of English* (London: His Majesty's Stationery Office, 1948), 43·
31.   Henri M. Peyre, op. cit., 133.
32.   Ibid., r64.
33.   Robert Alter, "Mimesis and the Motive for Fiction," *Images and Ideas in American Culture: The Functions of Criticism,* ed. Anhur Edelstein (1979; Hanover: Brandeis Univ. Press, 1981), 102.
34.   Ortega y Gasser, "Notes on the Novel," *The Dehumanization of Art and Other Writings on Art and Culture* (New York: Doubleday Anchor, 1956), 62.
35.   Robert Alter, op. cit., 104.
36.   Denis Donoghue, *The Arts Without Mystery* (Boston: Little, Brown, r983), 40.
37.   Jerry Speir, *Raymond Chandler* (New York: Frederick Ungar, 1981), 123-24.
38.   "Well, about the middle of September I don't see Regan any more. I don't notice it right away. You know how it is. A guy's there and you see him and then he ain't there and you don't not see him until something makes you think of it." Harry Jones to Philip Marlowe: *The Big Sleep* (1939; New York: Vintage Books, 1988), no 1.
39.   Jerry Speir, op. cit., nS-19.
40.   Raymond Chandler, "To Frederick Lewis Allen," May 7, 1948, *Selected Letters of Raymond Chandler,* ed. Frank MacShane (New York: Delta, 1981), 114.
41.   "Criticism is impossible in a world where the important thing is not to be right, or even to know the reasons for being right, but to write a column about a play ... which column however insignificant the ostensible subject, never lets down on the significance of the references to the subject." (Raymond Chandler, ibid., II{.) I suspect that Chandler would express a similar sentiment about critical readings of his own work and that of other detective fiction writers.
42.   James Naremore, op. cit., 61-3.
43.   Steven Marcus, op. cit., 202.
44.   Vincent B. Leitch, *American Literary Criticism from the Thirties to the Eighties* (New York: Columbia Univ. Press, 1988), 304.

45.   Walker Percy, "The Diagnostic Novel," *Harper's Magazine* June 1985: 39-45.
46.   Ralph Harper, *The World of Thrillers* (r969; Baltimore; Johns Hopkins Univ. Press, 1974) 128.
47.   Ayn Rand, "Bootleg Romanticism," *The Romantic A1anifesto: A Philosophy of Literature{I965;* New York: New American Library, 1971), 132.
48.   Ayn Rand, "What is Romanticism?" Ibid.,
49.   Ibid., 109-10.
50.   Raymond Chandler, "Casual Notes on the Mystery Novel," 1949, *Raymond Chandler Speaking,* ed. Dorothy Gardiner and Karhrine Sorley Walker (Boston: Houghton Miffiin, 1977), 63-70.

October 1990

Review: *Fascism and Theater*

The first time I watched a political convention to nominate and select presidential and vice-presidential candidates – I forget whether it was a Democratic or Republican one, it hardly mattered then, and does not matter now – I was astounded and not a little appalled by the sheer mindlessness of the event. There they were, hundreds of party delegates from all the states, a great slobbering mass worked up into consecutive bouts of noisy, frenzied rapture over supposedly charismatic nonentities whose platforms and speeches were measures of carefully crafted banality and skillfully inserted buzz words.

There they were, hundreds of adults of both sexes and various ages and sizes, wearing buttons and masks and funny hats and other goofy party paraphernalia, shouting and cheering themselves hoarse on cue in unison, forming conga lines and waving flags and signs, behaving as though they had all checked their brains, dignity and self-respect at the door. Which they evidently had. It was politics as a football game, it was a life-and-death matter of "our team" versus "their team" – all ideational content abandoned and replaced by raw emotion triggered by faces associated with particular sounds emptied of meaning.

The capacity for abandoning one's mind and for taking orders from delegate leaders has always seemed to be an important qualification for being a convention delegate. On the convention floor a delegate was and is still expected to surrender his "autonomous inner man" or individuality and merge into a smothering, communal *gestalt* with his party colleagues.

It is well known that television game show guests and contestants are selected for their quotient of enthusiasm and ability to communicate it to and with an audience. By this measure, a political convention has any game show beat by a factor of a thousand. And the prize is not a fancy car or living room set or a Caribbean cruise or $100,000, but the White House and "our guy" sitting in the Oval Office. In such escapist moments, when delegates seem to undergo a kind of mass "out of body" experience, the candidate is reduced to a mere symbolic image, regardless of character or qualification. He is "it." They become human counterparts of Pavlov's dogs, able to bark and drool and froth at the mouth on command and at the slightest autosuggestion by an overbearing delegate whip.

This is "democracy" in action. It was and still is stage-managed theater. It has not changed at all from the first time I saw a convention on black and white television. Being caught in the middle of such a phenomenon would be as scary to me as being surrounded by a mob of Muslims carrying signs that read "Behead those who insult Islam." One would be tempted to strike out at the maddened, sweating fools on the convention floor, only at the risk of being pummeled to death by delegates from Wisconsin and Idaho and Massachusetts and California. They would all plead temporary insanity, and get away with it.

After all, you had insulted their candidate, their Mahdi, their Thirteenth Imam. Their Savior. You deserved to die.

The religious hysteria, as an element of the phenomenon, is not coincidental, or an anomaly, or a fluke. It is part and parcel of modern convention behavior. It clearly was not a governing factor of the Constitutional Convention of 1787. Then, delegates brought their brains with them, they brought their principles and rectitude. Can you imagine the Founders wearing funny hats and chanting slogans and forming conga lines to press a point of Constitutional law? No? Is the contrast too ludicrous and obscene to contemplate? Yes. Each and every one of those men, even the villains and fence-sitters, was an exemplar of intellectual and moral decorum. Then look at the baboons and halfwits who are charged with selecting an individual whom they want to "run the country." Their choices over the last half century or more are reflections of what transpires on convention floors.

Today, the catalyst for the hysteria is not an invisible deity, but a flesh-and-blood human being. With calculated "behavioral" conditioning (*à la* B.F. Skinner), and a willingness to submerge one's identity in the collective, the sight and sound of a candidate can reduce these delegates to quivering masses of raw emotion. One almost expects them to fall to the convention floor, wreathing and shrieking in deliverance, and speaking in tongues like any Holy Roller. Call it Political Pentecostalism.

Reading *Fascism and Theatre: Comparative Studies on Aesthetics and Politics of Performance in Europe, 1925-1945**, I was not surprised to find in this collection of essays similarities between the methods employed by Nazis, Fascists and Communists to create and sustain support for their régimes, and the methods by which the Democrats and Republicans recruit and maintain their hard core, registered voters, activists and especially their convention delegates, the ones charged with nominating their parties' candidates – that is, the people responsible for foisting onto this country for the last half century or more a succession of fork-tongued demagogues and empty suits.

There are eighteen chapters in *Fascism and Theatre*, but only a few can be highlighted here. Some deal with the subject more successfully than others, but all discuss the role of "theater" in fascism. The term *fascism* is used generically in the essays to stand for Mussolini's Italian Fascism, Hitler's Nazism, and, to a lesser extent, General Francisco Franco's Falangist or Nationalist régime, which was a tepid admixture of Fascism and Nazism. (Although Spain remained "neutral" during World War II, Franco approved of sending approximately 19,000 Spanish volunteers to serve in a special division of the German army, to fight exclusively the "Bolsheviks" on the Eastern Front, but not the forces of Western armies. Spanish troops fought with the SS during the Soviet taking of Berlin.)

The term *theater* as used in the essays means either extravagant mass events such as the annual Nuremberg rallies or the political subornation of high and popular culture, from operas to plays to folk festivals to suit or conform to fascist aims and purposes.

One indisputable characteristic of fascism is that its theater borrowed heavily from Christian and especially Catholic practices and rituals, selectively exploiting the emotional nature of religion. Roger Griffin, in "Staging the Nation's Rebirth," introduces this idea which is elaborated on in most of the other essays:

> …[F]ascism, if it can seize power, is able to remain true to its core myth and legitimize itself only by generating an elaborate civic liturgy (or a 'civic,' or 'political' religion) based on the myth of imminent national rebirth. In the two cases where it managed to conquer the State, it rapidly developed characteristic rites and ceremonial, its own iconography and symbology, its own semiotic discourse, aping (but only aping) any established Church. [p. 25]

For Hitler and Germany, "rebirth" meant the resurrection of a Teutonic or Aryan state superior to all, and to rise from the ashes of the Versailles Treaty and the failed Weimar Republic; for Mussolini and Italy, it meant reviving the imperial grandeur of ancient Rome. Hitler and Mussolini, however, had first to concoct and propagate "myths" about the lost greatness of their countries, and then pose as saviors or messiahs who alone had the power to reclaim the greatness and lead their nations to glory. Propaganda ministries and bureaucracies were created in both countries to establish and enforce official party lines about a nation's past, present and future the subjects of art or in plays, national holidays, and even in opera.

Much of editor Günter Berghaus's contribution to the collection of essays, "The Ritual Core of Fascist Theatre: An Anthropological Perspective," is flawed by psycho-babble and sociological semiotics, but much of it also is lucid and on-point. To wit:

> Fascist parties rose to positions of power by gaining mass support and winning democratic elections. Millions of people were inspired by Mussolini and Hitler and developed a genuine enthusiasm for their politics, because they promised an answer to a need that was widely felt in different sections of the population. People were fascinated by what fascism proposed in response to a crisis that affected the economic, social and cultural spheres of their lives. Political promises played a role in this, but the *emotional appeal* of the leaders and their programs was probably stronger. Fascist leaders avoided the *rational rhetorics* typical of bourgeois politicians, and instead employed *performative language* that had a captivating force unequalled by traditional means of propaganda. {pp. 39-40. *Italics* mine.]

Sound familiar? Does that passage hark back to the 2008 presidential campaign and election? Does it not describe the method by which the current occupant of the White House rose to power? However, Berghaus correctly dwells on the relationship between the religious and secular elements of fascism.

> This grafting of the Christian redeemer and savior image onto a historical person was a post-figuration technique often employed in the Christian drama of the Baroque period and was ultimately derived from medieval theology. Both Hitler and Mussolini were well versed in the literary traditions of Christian religion and were fully capable of adopting their conventions. Hitler helped the transformation of his own person into the archetypal, divine redeemer figure through his mythological biography, *Mein Kampf.* [p. 62]

Berghaus quotes Hitler on the purpose of the Party rallies held in Nuremberg and other German cities. From *Mein Kampf.*

> Mass meetings are a necessity because the individual (...) who feels isolated and easily succumbs to the fear of loneliness, is given here an idea of a greater community. (...) When he as a seeker is swept along by the mighty effect of the ecstasy and

enthusiasm of three to four thousand others, when the visible success and agreement of thousands confirm to him the rightness of the new doctrine (...), then he will submit to the magic spell of what we call "mass suggestiveness." The will, the longing, as well as the power of thousands of people are accumulated in every individual. The man who entered such a meeting doubting and wavering leaves it with an inner conviction: he has become a member of a community. [p. 60]

One could also say that this was no less true for Hitler, that he was literally nothing if not the leader of such a community. Without all those chanted "Sieg Heils" and tens of thousands looking up at him on a high rostrum with adoration and worship, he was a vacuum, an isolated and fearful nonentity who assumed an identity only in the presence and eyes of disciplined and attentive mobs.

> Many uninvolved contemporary observers were struck by the fact that the public rituals of fascist régimes were "more than a gorgeous show; [they] also had something of the mysticism and religious fervor of an Easter or Christmas mass in a great cathedral." "Is this a dream or reality?" asked one of the visitors to the *Reichsparteitag* 1936 after the spectacle on the Zeppelinwiese and concluded: "It is like a majestic church service (*Andacht*) where we have congregated to find new strength..."

> [Albert] Speer said that Hitler canonized the formations, processions and celebrations so that "they were almost like rites of the founding of a Church." Once he had worked out the right forms, he wanted to fix them as "unalterable rites" that gave him the status of a "founder of a religion." [p. 53]

Mussolini was of a like mind concerning the religious "experience" possible in the Italian version.

> Mussolini stated in 1923 that "Fascism is a religious phenomenon of vast historical proportions" and that fascism was "a civic and political belief, but also a religion, a militia, a spiritual discipline, which has had – like Christianity – its confessors, its testifying witnesses, its saints." The Fascist Party was often described as "a new Church (*La nuova chiesa* is the title, for example, of a play by [Virgilio] Caselli) or as a "religious or military order." [pp. 53-54]

For example, from 1933 on, from Hitler's assumption of the chancellorship through the next eleven or so years, German playwrights (those who prostituted their talents to the Party) wrote plays that portrayed the past struggle of the German people to assume their "rightful" place in the world. If this meant fudging history or ascribing to past historical persons presaging yearnings for Nazi or Fascist domination and identity, such hacks were perfectly willing to falsify history, submit their work to Party censors and make the requisite changes. As Berghaus notes:

> Consequently, fascist playwrights evoked a large number of situations that indicated a return to a united people. They propagated a new ethics that was aimed at *overcoming egotism*, uniting one individual with other individuals, creating a firm bond between them, making them identify with the aims of the fascist State and submit to the orders of a leader....The conduct of this leader was modeled, of course, on the historical examples given by the Führer, Duce, and Caudillo. Or rather, one should say, on the way those historical figures were mythisised, legendised and sanctified in fascist hagiography. [p. 61. *Italics* mine.]

Neither Hitler nor Mussolini was ever portrayed in these plays. Some species of false but more likely fearful fastidiousness in Party censors prohibited it; no actor could have been trusted to faultlessly impersonate Hitler or Mussolini, even had a hack written a play that featured them, and probably no actor would have wished to risk the role, either. Hitler and Mussolini were instead substituted with stand-ins or proxies, such as Frederick the Great or Bismarck or Garibaldi or some two-dimensional fictional character, always ready to sacrifice himself for the greater good in the most cavalierly selfless manner, which was the unity of the German or Italian people. Acceptable plays were set in the past, to convey a false historical overture to Nazism or Fascism – or the alleged inexorable inevitability of Nazism and Fascism, which a mere individual was helpless to oppose and whose only recourse was to submit to it.

Barbara Panse, in her essay, "Censorship in Nazi Germany: The Influence of the Reich's Ministry of Propaganda on German Theater and Drama, 1933-1945," discusses several of these plays, and cites how one playwright even perverted the American Revolution:

> In Hanns Johst's play [*Thomas Paine*], Thomas Paine is the ideological Führer of the American War of Independence. He, too, upholds the notions of colonialism and conquest. With the propagandistic slogan, "America needs land," he seeks to mobilize

the exhausted and hungry insurgent army so that they venture to take the path into the unknown, to victory or death. His appeal to faith and comradeship forges the "racially worthy citizens" (*volkisch wertvollen Glieder*) of America into a nation. In this play, the life of the Führer character also ends tragically, but his mission is fulfilled: the 'national idea' has come to fruition. [p. 149]

Johst wrote this play in 1927. He was a career anti-Semite who wrote a play, *Schlageter*, which extolled Nazi ideology, to celebrate Hitler's victory and birthday in 1933. It is interesting to note also that Howard Fast, a steadfast member of the American Communist Party, also appropriated the American Revolution as a means to advance the "people's struggle" narrative (*à la* Howard Zinn) on the origins of the United States. *Citizen Tom Paine* (1943) is one of a number of novels he wrote set in that period.

No discussion of the theatrics of fascism would be complete without mentioning Leni Riefenstahl's documentary, *Triumph of the Will*. This task fell to contributor Hans-Ulrich Thamer and his essay, "The Orchestration of the National Community: The Nuremberg Party Rallies of the NSDAP." Writing about the purpose and style of the rallies, Thamer observes about the 1934 Nazi Party Congress:

> The heroic style and dramaturgy of the event were fixed on celluloid by Leni Riefenstahl in her film *Triumph of the Will* (1934). Much more than simply a documentary, this film foregrounded the symbolism and liturgy of the ceremonies and established their pattern for the years to come. At the same time, the film disseminated the mass spectacle of Nuremberg throughout Germany. It was a "production of a production" and thereby a reduplication of the "mass appeal" of National Socialist political aesthetics. *Triumph of the Will* turned the military parade of the National Socialist movement into a platform for the Führer-cult. [p. 175]

Thamer then takes the reader on a tour of the typical succeeding rallies, all based on what Riefenstahl had recorded in 1934, which acted as a template, and then were expanded in scope and in the number of participants. These rallies lasted for days. Thamer follows Hitler from elevated rostrum to a ceremony of flags and banners when he rubbed shoulders and pressed flesh with rank-and-file, to a ritual of consecration of the "martyrs" that was much like a glorified mass of the dead. Hitler was the focal point of every important event. But, it was all a manufactured show.

> Nothing was left to chance in the stage-management of the Nuremberg rallies. Every stylistic device had a purpose. The flags were determined in number, size and position; shortcomings in the urban development and gaps in the old town fortifications were covered up by scenery. Everything was subjected to the meticulous plans of the bureaucratic and technical apparatus. The men in charge of the cult were cool-headed technicians, sons of a rational era. Yet they were also theatrical wizards who knew intuitively how to exploit age-old cultic practices for their political aims. It was exactly this link between atavistic ideology, mystical ceremony and the modern age, which helped to *eliminate all critical reasoning in both audience and participants.* [p. 186. *Italics mine.*]

Before the entire length of *Triumph of the Will* was removed from YouTube for copyright infringement (the full version now can be watched with ads), I watched it twice, and I can attest to the effectiveness of the stage management described by Thamer. I distinctly remember Jimmy Carter's appearance at the conclusion of the 1976 Democratic Convention, when he and his wife Rosalind appeared on stage before a brilliant blue background. That was calculation.

The typical American political convention is also planned and laid out in meticulous detail, from the flags and bunting, to the timed applause and cheers, to the demonstrations of dancing and chanting, to the bands and choreography and lighting, all the way to the climax of the acceptance speeches. Little during these cattle calls could be called spontaneous, except for the essential emotional character of the proceedings that verges on a mass revival meeting. But the spontaneity is also cued and calculated to advance or obstruct a point of order or dissension. For the typical delegate, a convention is a vacation from reality, from the facts of political and economic life.

I doubt that many delegates, upon returning home from a *Grand Gestalt,* pause long enough to acknowledge just how much they have degraded themselves and regret having let loose a monster. And the ensuing political campaigns have become more and more shallow and meaningless popularity contests, with candidates stooping to the level of rock stars repeating the most popular lyrics and buzz words. Thamer concludes his essay with:

The Führer-myth as the propagandist core of the rally distracted from the political reality of Party as well as everyday life and became the most important means of stabilizing the rule of the Nazi Party. The dream world conjured up by the events manipulated consciousness and created a second reality, which of course could not change the outside world, but could counteract and control it. [p. 188.]

The Obama/McCain campaigns of 2008 were also products of such dream worlds, the one more masterfully managed and staged than the other. And then the winner encountered the "outside world" and, like King Canute, as the legend goes, he attempted to command its tides to cease. In fact, Canute was making a point for his supporters, that he was only a king and not a miracle worker. Perhaps Obama will be imbued with the same wisdom.

The Republicans, however, seem determined to offer their own Æthelred the Unready to oppose him. Election year 2012 is going to be interesting.

*Providence/Oxford: Berghahn Books: 1996. Edited by Günter Berghaus.

December 2011

§ Finis §

www.ingramcontent.com/pod-product-compliance
Lightning Source LLC
Chambersburg PA
CBHW070650290526
45790CB00001B/263